D.H. Lawrence

Etruscan Places

Foreword by Massimo Pallottino

nuova immagine editrice (Siena)

First published as *Etruscan Places* by Martin Secker, London 1932

[ISBN 88 7145 080 9]

© 1986, nuova immagine editrice
via San Quirico, 13 – I-53100 Siena

tel. 0577 - 42.625
fax 0577 - 44.633

First edition: 1986
Second edition: 1994
Third edition: 1997

Designed by Auro Lecci, Florence
Phototypeset by Leadercomp, Florence
Photolithography by Mani, Florence
Printed in Italy by Centrooffset, Siena

CONTENTS

DAVID HERBERT LAWRENCE (1885-1930), one of the greatest English novelists of the century, was born at Eastwood in Nottinghamshire and died of tuberculosis at Vence, in Provence. Together with his wife Frieda von Richtofen he lived and travelled for long periods in Italy: at Gargnano on Lake Garda and at Lerici (*Twilight in Italy* 1912-13), at Capri, Sardinia and Taormina (*Sea and Sardinia* 1920-22), where he translated *Mastro don Gesualdo* and the *Novelle Rusticane* of Verga. After long periods in Ceylon and, above all, in Mexico, Lawrence returned to Italy, first to Spotorno, and finally to the Villa Mirenda at Scandicci (1926-28). The first edition of *Lady Chatterley's Lover* is also Florentine, published privately by Pino Orioli in his «Lungarno Series» (1928). *Etruscan Places* is of the same period, a brilliant and detailed account of his travels in Etruria in April 1927, accompanied by his friend Earl Brewster, an American painter.

There are dowsers, whose hazel wands will tremble, not only for water, but also for gold and bronze and iron, even for bones or an urn-full of human dust. Archaeologists have used these mysteriously gifted persons as the truffle-hunter uses his dog or his learned sow, to nose out the buried treasures of ancient cemeteries or long deserted cities - used them, it is reported, with what are, sometimes, the happiest results. But the mere locating of treasure is not enough; we demand to know the significance of what is dug up; we ask when and how and why. The archaeologist applies his scientific method to the solution of the problem. So far as the when and the how are concerned, this method is entirely satisfactory. But when it comes to the inner why, the results, in many cases, are not so good. It is at this point that the man of science might well be advised to invoke the aid of another kind of dowser - a dowser of the psychological rather than the material plane, a diviner, not of water or metals, but of feelings, motives, beliefs.

Such a psychological diviner was D.H. Lawrence. He was a man extraordinarily sensitive to the life that is buried in every fragment of matter. He felt its quality and its intensity, as the dowser feels the quantity and the subterranean distance of the water or the metal which moves his twig of hazel. In the six chapters of *Etruscan Places* - chapters complete in themselves, but forming only a part of the longer study of Etruscan civilization which he projected, but was unable to carry out - Lawrence has left us the results of his dowsing expeditions in the tombs of Cerveteri and Tarquinia and Vulci, among the vases and the carved sarcophagi of Volterra. The record of this journey through modern Italian space and Etruscan time is not only a beautiful and delicate work of literary art; it also make a real contribution to historical knowledge. For Lawrence has felt his way into the minds of the Etruscans. What he says about their ways of thinking and feeling and being is, I am convinced, fundamentally true. There is no proving its truth, of course. But any sensitive person who has looked at the painted tombs of Tarquinia and who reads what Lawrence has to say about the culture which produced them, is left with the inner certainty that Lawrence's interpretation is right.

Aldous Huxley
Spectator 4/11/1932

The essay by Massimo Pallottino, Professor of Etruscology and Italian Antiquities at the University of Rome, President of the Institute of Italian and Etruscan Studies, is the text presented at a conference of the Associazione Culturale Italiana on the 18th January, 1957 and published as *Scienza e poesia alla scoperta dell'Etruria* in *Quaderni A.C.I.*, vol.24, 1957. It is reproduced here by kind permission of the author.

IN SEARCH OF ETRURIA: SCIENCE AND THE IMAGINATION
by Massimo Pallottino

Res ardua, vetustis novitatem dare, novis auctoritatem,
obsoletis nitorem, obscuris lucem, fastiditis gratiam, dubis
fidem, omnibus vero naturam, et naturae suae omnia.

«It is no easy matter to give novelty to old subjects,
authority to new, to impart lustre to rusty things, light to the
obscure and mysterious, to throw a charm over what is
distasteful, to command credence for doubtful matters, to give
nature to everything, and to arrange everything according to
its nature.»

A hundred years ago George Dennis opened his travelogue
on the Etruscan world by citing these words of the Elder Pliny in
the preface to his work, which still remains even today the
liveliest and most deservedly celebrated yet to have been written
on ancient Etruria.

I recall and repeat them in opening this piece of my own
because I feel they sum up and almost startlingly anticipate the
difficulties facing anyone who attempts to define the Etruscan
problem; anyone, that is, who aspires to trace the course which
Etruscology has taken, or, rather, who attempts to grasp in their
essentials modern ideas and impressions of Etruscan civilization.

In truth, as far as I am aware, there is no other aspect or
segment of ancient history which has so strangely teased the
learned, roused such furious controversy among them, and
drawn such varied, amazing and extraordinary reactions among
the cultured in modern times, as this topic of the history of the
ancient Etruscans.

The difficulty of interpreting meagre, bare and ambiguous
data, the influence of classical sources, uncertainties and confli-
cts in research methodology - all these factors from the very
outset made even specialist scholars abandon the steady calm
and investigative serenity which are particularly indispensable in
approaching such a problematical task. Rivers of ink have
flowed and still flow in bitter polemic, in categorical statements,

in sudden reversals of judgement on such red herrings as the question of the origin of the Etruscans, whilst far more important points were and still are often left in shadow, neglected and unexplored.

The discord and, at times, outright disbelief among specialists about each other's findings also opens the floodgates to studies by amateurs which pour out regularly in due season. We've all heard their earth-shaking revelations; Mr. Tom, Engineer Dick, or Canon Harry has at last succeeded in deciphering Etruscan; the riddle has been solved; there's a sensation in the press, public interest and gratification. Then, slowly, silence descends, and the incident sinks into oblivion, only to start up all over again some years, or even some months, later.

The public at large gets passionately involved, it goes from the hot douche of enthusiasm to the cold douche of disillusionment, but still 'loves' its Etruscans. People have formed their own image of them, made them almost into a legend, or a series of legends, often quite at variance with what has been factually ascertained, sustained rather by the reflections of the imaginative writer. These legends, in essence, fulfil the need for escapist fantasy-activity and keep alive a sense of mystery. Even when the haze of mystery shows signs of lifting, our imaginative contemporary public steadfastly withholds all belief, as if an achieved certainty would break the spell of the imaginary enigma and, little by little, prosaically, reduce that zone of the irrational in which our contemporaries delight in taking secret refuge whenever possible.

Let us, for instance, consider the language question. People are roughly aware that there are few original texts and that they are not of much interest, being mostly brief sepulchral or votive inscriptions; that we lack any external key to their meaning, such as dictionaries or bilingual texts; that Etruscan has no direct affinity with other tongues known to the ancient world, such as to permit effective comparisons to be made. Yet, as far back as two hundred years ago, the savants of the eighteenth century had substantially succeeded in reading the Etruscan inscriptions, identifying the sounds of most of the characters which are derived from the Greek. They had identified the proper names of persons and deities. They had even established the meaning of several words and translated the simpler texts. The patient efforts of succeeding generations of scholars, after many ups and downs, developed these early achievements, bringing us to our present state of knowledge. Etruscan writing has now been comprehensively studied. The essential features of the phonetic and grammatical structures of the language have been laid bare. The number of words whose meaning is known with certainty or with a high degree of probability has grown. The longer and more difficult texts have been subjected to analysis. In truth, we can today read with almost perfect understanding the overwhelming majority of Etruscan inscriptions and at least guess at the meaning of the more complex religious texts, such as the manuscript of the winding-sheet of the Zagreb Mummy and the Capua tile, even though many words and many passages remain obscure. And further progress can be expected within the not too distant future.

But, as the legend has it among the public at large, Etruscan still defies decipherment or interpretation as it did up to two centuries ago. The riddle of Etruscan is in fact the riddle of riddles, the Sphinx with a capital S. A Sphinx that has not spoken, because it cannot, for if it gave away its secret it would no longer be a sphinx, and that would be the end of the enchanting dream.

Two years ago I delivered a lecture on the present state of our knowledge about the Etruscan language, talking about the positive achievements I have just listed, and I had the impression that my audience were listening with great interest. But when the lecture was over, quite a few people approached me either to express amazement or disillusionment or actually to declare that, no, Etruscan still remained for them, all in all, indecipherable and incomprehensible. No less curious is the fact that many journalists of different nationalities, wishing to attract the public to visit the Exhibition of Etruscan Art and Civilization, which demonstrated the progress of scientific research into every aspect including the linguistic, particularly emphasized, even in their reports and articles, the glamorous mystery of the indecipherable and unintelligible Etruscan language.

I don't think there is any other field of human knowledge in which there is such a daft cleavage between what has been scientifically ascertained and the unshakeable beliefs of the public. In the past, this absurdity used to exasperate me. With the rigour and the almost puritanical intransigence of a young scholar, I was impelled to regard it as a symptom of incredible and widespread ignorance. Then, little by little, I began to take an interest in the phenomenon as such, as a 'cultural' phenome-

*non, which exists, and for which there must be an explanation.
To put it down to «ignorance» would be too facile. Why on
earth should the Etruscans so uniquely inspire such a tradition of
ignorance - a tradition so deep rooted, so far-flung, so tenacious,
so blithe and self-assured, so proof against any suggestion, any
correction, any instruction?*

*The truth lies elsewhere. The truth is that this world of
contemporary popular legends about the Etruscans, this very
intense and widespread passion for things Etruscan which has
drawn hundreds of thousands of visitors to the halls of the
Exhibition which has recently been open to the public in
Europe's chief cities; which attracts contemporary artists to the
line and colour of Etruscan art; which feeds Etruscan motifs to
craftsmen and fashion-designers: this unique and manifold
phenomenon has no connection with scholarship, science or the
scientific mentality, because it fulfils quite different needs, it
springs from quite different sources of inspiration, it subsists in a
sphere of its own, it has a truth of its own which is not that of
science, but rather of the imagination.*

*There is in fact a scholars' Etruria and a writers' Etruria,
deriving from two divergent and, in a sense, non-communicating
traditions; one, that of objective enquiry; the other, that of
poetic intuition.*

*The scholars' Etruria has followed the path of consecutive
reasoning, moving from the concrete data provided by ancient
sources or by archaeological investigation so as to achieve, on
the basis of the critical interpretation of those data, a reconstru-
ction as organic and historically faithful as possible of the
political, cultural, and economic experience of the Etruscans,
their language, their thinking, their customs, their figurative art.
Our established knowledge is now immensely greater, more
certain and better ordered than it was a hundred or two hundred
years ago. This is not only due to the wealth of evidence turned
up by fresh excavations, but also - and supremely - to more
refined methods and the general advance in the science of
antiquity. Despite the lack of first-hand historical evidence, and
within the limits imposed by that lack, the lineaments of the
Etruscan people are sufficiently discernible within the panorama
of ancient Italy, somewhere in between the Greek experience and
the Roman, linked to Mediterranean traditions and containing
elements which anticipate and help to prompt the rise of a new
European civilization. For the scholar, then, there are no*

'mysteries'; open problems, yes, no more numerous and complex, though, than those encountered in exploring other regions
and other civilizations of antiquity.

The writers' Etruria was born into the Romantic era and was
the child of Romanticism. It crystallizes, transmits and trans-
forms into a poetic truth the emotions experienced by modern
humanity when confronted with the revelation of a new face of
the ancient world, with the great explorations of the Etruscan
necropoles which took place at the beginning of the nineteenth
century. Europe had up to then dreamed the classical dream of a
stately and statuesque antiquity - the dream of Winckelmann and
Visconti, of Thorvaldsen and Canova. But abruptly the Maremma disclosed its treasures. Out of the land around Vulci poured
myriads of painted vases. On the walls of the sepulchral
chambers of Tarquinia appeared frescoes throbbing with life.
Cerveteri displayed the barbaric splendour of its oriental gold.
Colour, movement, exotic images, manifestations of a spontaneous and immediate reality sprang out in contrast to the white
marble and the idealizations of the academic canon. Archaeological passion rushed out of the chilly halls of the great Neo-
Classical museums and into the sunshine, into the wild scrubland
and rock of the Campagna. The initiative passed out of the
hands of the court antiquaries into those of the enthusiastic
explorers and rough-and-ready riflers of tombs. Erudition
turned into adventure.

The romance of Etruria begins at this point, with fanciful
broodings over its landscapes, its ruins, its history and its mystery. Certain basic themes are established, certain favoured
motifs upon which modern literature will muse and embroider.
The cues are already there in that extraordinary vision of the re-
emerging Etruscan world that was The Cities and Cemeteries of
Etruria by George Dennis, British Consul in Rome, traveller,
antiquary and chronicler of his times. Its progress is to be
followed, in the wake of the success of Dennis' book, through
the works of recent English writers, from D.H. Lawrence's
Etruscan Places to the stories of Aldous Huxley.

The first motifs through which writers approach Etruria so
as to transfigure it is that of the landscape. All of us even today,
despite the tide of agricultural and industrial development which
is invading the desolate silences of the Maremma, have
experienced unique emotions in travelling along the ravines of
Norchia, thick with brambles, among wild olives, mastic bushes,

myrtles, along high banks of red volcanic tufa out of which innumerable tombs open their mouths and fantastic buildings are outlined, with perhaps a few rooks circling against the azure sky; or in gazing by the light of the setting sun at the hills of Tarquinia softly undulating like a green sea of wheat; or in halting atop the Arx of Populonia, sitting beside the gigantic blocks of its Etruscan ramparts, hung with ivy, with the sea glittering opposite and the pale-blue outline of the Isle of Elba.

One can easily imagine the quantity and quality of the impressions which this picturesque land of Etruria must have evoked in the minds of its visitors at a time when enormous tracts were uninhabited, making more stirring than it is today the contrast between the wilderness and, breaking through here and there, the remains of Etruria's long vanished civilization.

Carducci, a son of maritime Etruria, has in a few brief lines given us a swift and coruscating image of it, redolent of ancestral connections, which, more profoundly than any other, captures the feeling of immensity, mutability and death. He addresses the «roan courser» of his song:

> Do you recall the widowed shores of the Tuscan main
>   where, bowed over the sown and cloudy plain,
>   the feudal tower,
>
> with its long shadow of tedium, from the dark scorched hills
>   guards Rasena's cities amid the woods slumbering still
>   in the grave's power,
>
> whilst wearily parching, punishing sirocco mocks
>   the thirst of the wild figs swaying atop the massive four-
>   square blocks
> green between sea and sky,
>
> atop those huge blocks whence the watchful Tyrrhenian trader
>   awaited the red Phoenician sails amid the azure,
>   which he hoped to descry?
>
> Do you recall Populonia, and Roselle? ...

One of the unique effects of the Etruscan landscape is that of
fusing together in one indissoluble impression of beauty both
natural characteristics and the traces of human activity: rocks,
plants, ancient and medieval ruins, present-day dwellings,
almost as if the handiwork of history, under time's usury, had
gradually reverted to nature's living womb. So that one often
wonders whether this stone or that has recently been moved by
latter-day builders or by the people of the Middle Ages or by the
Romans or the Etruscans, or by mythic Titans, or by God.

These are the words in which Dennis described the famous
Abbadia bridge at Vulci:

> The castle stands on the verge of a deep ravine which is
> here spanned by a narrow bridge, fenced in with parapets so
> tall as to block all view. Not till I had crossed it had I any idea
> of its character; and then, from the slope below, it burst on
> me like a fresh creation. It is verily a magnificent structure,
> bestriding the rocky abyss like a colossus, with the Fiora
> fretting and foaming at a vast depth beneath. But what means
> this extraordinary curtain of stalactites which overhangs the
> bridge on this side, depending in huge jagged masses from the
> parapet, and looking as though a vast cataract had rolled over
> the top of the bridge, and been petrified in its fall, ere it could
> reach the ground? One might almost fancy the bridge had
> been hewn out of the solid rock, and that the workmen had
> abandoned it before its completion, - like Michelangelo
> statues with unfinished extremities. ... The solemn castle, high
> on the cliff by its side, rearing its dark-red tower against the
> sky - the slopes clothed with the ilex and shrubs - the huge
> masses of rock in the hollow - the stream struggling and
> boiling through the narrow cleft - the steep frowning cliffs
> seen through the arch - are so many accessories in keeping
> with the principal object, forming with it as striking and
> picturesque a scene as I remember in Etruria (1883 ed. I; 44
> 2-3).

This intermingling of nature and history is most vivid in
Lawrence's poetic prose, intensified almost to morbidity in his
sensibility towards flowers among the ruins, exalted to a cosmic
lyricism of atmosphere, colour and light. So in the necropolis of
Cerveteri:

> There is a stillness and a softness in these great grassy
> mounds with their ancient stone girdles, and down the central
> walk there lingers still a kind of homeliness and happiness.

True, it was a still and sunny afternoon in April, and larks
rose from the soft grass of the tombs. But there was a stillness
and a soothingness in all the air, in that sunken place, and a
feeling that it was good for one's soul to be there.

And so on the bluffs of Volterra:

> From time to time, going up to the town homewards, we
> come to the edge of the walls and look out into the vast glow
> of gold, which is sunset, marvellous, the steep ravines sinking
> in darkness, the farther valley silently, greenly gold, with hills
> breathing luminously up, passing out into the pure, sheer gold
> gleams of the far-off sea, in which a shadow, perhaps an
> island, moves like a mote of life. And like great guardians the
> Carrara mountains jut forward, naked in the pure light like
> flesh, with their crests portentous: so that they seem to be
> advancing on us: while all the vast concavity of the west roars
> with gold liquescency, as if the last hour had come, and the
> gods were smelting us all back into yellow transmuted
> oneness.

*This dreamworld is inhabited by folk full of character,
whom the hyperborean traveller scans with eager eye, as if
searching there for the imprint of those other mysterious folk
who now slumber deep in their rock-tombs. The theme of latter-
day ethnography, of the* Volkspsychologie *of the inhabitants of
Tuscany and Northern Latium, is one of the richest and most
stimulating in the pages of Dennis and Lawrence, which presents
an animated kaleidoscope of extremely vivid characters, skilfully
drawn, sometimes unforgettable. Their sympathy goes sponta-
neously, as is always the case with writers from northern
Europe, to the humblest characters: inn-keepers and landladies,
attendants at ancient monuments, impromptu guides, country
folk, herdsmen; all of whom also seem at times to merge with
the colour of their untamed land. In dealing with the gentry or
middle-class people, the description lingers most appreciatively
on the vigorous country gentlemen, lovers of good earth and
good wine, like that* gonfaloniere *(meaning 'major') of Corneto
to whom we owe some of the most famous archaeological finds
from the Tarquinia necropolis in the first half of the last century
and who is thus portrayed by Dennis:*

> When I first visited Corneto, I had the advantage of the
> guidance of Signor Carlo Avvolta, the *gonfaloniere* or chief

magistrate of the town. He was a lively, intelligent, old gentleman, experienced in excavations, deeply interested in the antiquities of this his birthplace, ever ready to impart information, and displaying as much courtesy to strangers as cordiality to his friends. He might be consulted with profit also on the more rousing matters of Maremma sports. Though nearly eighty years of age, he was still a keen sportsman, and entered on the fatigues and perils of the chase with the ardour of a man of thirty. Wherever his activity might lead him during the day, in the evening he was sure to be found at the *caffè*, or at the *spezieria*, where we would descant, with all the enthusiasm of his nature, on the last boar or roe-buck he had made to bite the dust, or on the paintings and furniture of Etruscan tombs (1883 ed., I; 304-305).

When Lawrence, eighty years later, retraced Dennis's Etruscan itinerary, such patriarchal and benign authorities no longer existed. Their breed had vanished forever. But even lesser folk has grown less serene and trusting, or had been transfigured into symbols. Anyone who has read the first essay in Etruscan Places *will remember the extraordinary apparition of the faun-man in the tavern at Cerveteri:*

Into the cavern swaggers a spurred shepherd wearing goat-skin trousers with the long, rusty brown goat's hair hanging shaggy from his legs. He grins and drinks wine, and immediately one sees again the shaggy-legged faun. His face is a faun-face, not deadened by morals. He grins quietly, and talks very subduedly, shyly, to the fellow who draws the wine from the barrels. It is obvious fauns are shy, very shy, especially of moderns like ourselves. He glances at us from a corner of his eye, ducks, wipes his mouth on the back of his hand, and is gone, clambering with his hairy legs on to his lean pony, swirling, and rattling away with a neat little clatter of hoofs, under the ramparts and away to the open. He is the faun escaping again out of the city precincts, far more shy and evanescent than any Christian virgin. You cannot hard-boil him.

Racial continuity is a reality inscribed on the faces of the living as in the strata of the sepulchral cities. But for Dennis the European as for Carducci the Italian, it unfolded through the centuries without rancour:

Here at the foot of the hill slumber those Umbrian forefathers
who first broke
with the ring of axes your sacred silences, oh Appennine:
here slumber the Etruscans who came down with war-
trumpet, with lance, with eyes,
set steady high on your mysterious slopes,
and the great ruddy Celts rushing to rinse off the carnage
in the cold mountain waters they greeted as Reno,
and the noble race of Rome, and the long-haired
Lombard,
who was the last to camp upon the wooden heights.
They slumber with the latest of our people.

Thus the poet mused at the Charterhouse at Bologna. But, for the English Lawrence, racial continuity is a well defined and polemical reality. He discovers and loves in the modern Italians the fresh vitality of the ancient Italians and, above all, of the Etruscans; but he hates the Romans, the «Prussians» of antiquity, to whom he imputes the crime of having crushed under their iron steel the splendid ancient flower of Etruria. This is a note that Lawrence might have culled from the tail-enders of eighteen-century Etruscomania, particularly from Giuseppe Micali, who, well into the nineteenth century, turned out a windy, anti-Roman history of Italy. But Micali's ingeniously erudite approach turns, in Lawrence, into the pattern of myth, into the incandescent matter of a symbolic historical drama:

> Because a fool kills a nightingale with a stone, is he therefore greater than the nightingale? Because the Roman took the life out of the Etruscan, was he therefore greater than the Etruscan? Not he! Rome fell, and the Roman phenomenon with it. Italy today is far more Etruscan in its pulse than Roman; and will always be so. The Etruscan element is like the grass of the field and the sprouting of corn, in Italy: it will always be so.

Ancient Etruria, in fact, for the English writers of recent generations, seems to have been transfigured into the idea of a lost world, happy by nature, impetuously alive with spontaneous physical life, untrammelled by reason or morality: a world, precisely, which was progressively stifled down the century by reason and morality, to the misfortune of mankind .

> *The things they did, in their easy centuries, are as natural and as easy as breathing. They leave the breast breathing freely and pleasantly, with a certain fullness of life. Even the tombs. And that is the true Etruscan quality: ease, naturalness, and an abundance of life, no need to force the mind or the soul in any direction. ... The natural flowering of life! It is not so easy for human beings as it sounds. Behind all the Etruscan liveliness was a religion of life, which the chief men were seriously responsible for. Behind all the dancing was a vision, and even a science of life. ... We have lost the art of living; and in that most important science of all, the science of daily life, the science of behaviour, we are complete ignoramuses. We have psychology instead.*

But what is this Etruscan vitality that glows from those fleshy images frescoed in the tombs of Tarquinia but the bursting forth of sexual energy free from the constraints of deadening inhibitions. The author of Lady's Chatterley's Lover saw this imaginative vision as being also a symbolic and emotional issue, matter for scathing polemic against his contemporaries:

> here all is plain, simple, usually with no decoration, and with those easy natural proportions whose beauty one hardly notices, they come so naturally, physically. It is the natural beauty of proportion of the phallic consciousness, contrasted with the more studied or ecstatic proportion of the mental and spiritual Consciousness we are accustomed to.

Certain images which Dennis had labelled obscene hold, for Lawrence:

> The same naive wonder as the rest, the same archaic innocence, accepting life, knowing all about it, and *feeling* the meaning, which is like a stone fallen into consciousness, sending its rings ebbing out and out, to the extremes. The two little pictures have a symbolic meaning, quite distinct from a *moral* meaning - or an immoral. The words moral and immoral have no force. ...
> Besides, the Etruscan were vicious. We know it, because their enemies and exterminators said so. Just as we knew the unspeakable depths of *our* enemies in the late war. Who isn't vicious to his enemy? To my detractors I am a very effigy of vice. *A la bonne heure!*...Myself, however, if the Etruscans

were vicious, I'm glad they were. To the Puritan all things are
impure, as somebody says. And those naughty neighbours of
the Romans at least escaped being Puritans.

*The writers' Etruria now follows the flight of pure fantasy:
from interpretation it has turned into transfiguration, from
transfiguration into symbol, from symbol into paradox. But in
one unforgettable scene of Huxley's* Those Barren Leaves *it
actually becomes the subject of arabesque, of sheer fun, of a
refined and uninhibited intellectual conjuring trick. The writer
has assembled his characters in an imaginary Etruscan tomb
which, by an intentionally magical effect, combines within itself
the features and images of the chief painted tombs in the
Tarquinia necropolis.*

Mr. Cardan had beckoned to the guide. 'Bring the lamp a
little nearer', he said in Italian, and when the light had been
approached, he went on slowly spelling out the primitive
Greek writing on the wall of the tomb: *flucuthuck nun* ... - (*it
does not seem to matter if the text of this 'inscription' does not
really exist in Tarquinia*). He straightened himself up. 'Charming language' he said, 'charming! Ever since I learned that
the Etruscans used to call the god of wine *Fufluns*, I've taken
the keenest interest in their language. Fufluns - how incompa-
rably more appropriate that is than Bacchus, or Liber, or
Dionysos! Fufluns, *Fufluns*,' he repeated with delighted em-
phasis. 'It couldn't be better. They had a real linguistic genius,
those creatures. What poets they must have produced!... It's a
great language, I insist, a great language. Who knows? A
couple of generations hence some new Busby or Keat may be
drumming Etruscan syntax and Etruscan prosody into the
backsides of British boyhood. Nothing would give me greater
satisfaction. Latin and Greek have a certain infinitesimal
practical value. But Etruscan is totally and absolutely useless.
What better basis for a gentleman's education could possibly
be discovered? It's the great dead language of the future. If
Etruscan didn't exist, it would be necessary to invent it.'

*He is faced with the objection that the school-teacher would
have little to impart, given that there is no Etruscan literature.
But Cardan retorts:*

'So much the better,' replied Mr. Cardan. 'If we wrote it

ourselves, we might find Etruscan literature interesting. Etruscan literature composed by Etruscans would be as boring as any other ancient literature. But if the epics were written by you, the Socratic dialogues by me, the history by some master of fiction like Miss Thriplow - then we'd possess a corpus in which the rare schoolboys who can derive some profit from their education could take a real interest. And when, a generation hence, we have become as much out of date in our ideas as Tully or Horace, the literature of Etruria will be rewritten by our descendants. Each generation will use the dead language to express its own ideas. And expressed in so rich an idiom as I take Etruscan to be, the ideas will seem the more significant and memorable.'

After debating whether the Etruscan word flucuthukh *means 'soda water' or 'love', Cardan holds forth on the diverse forms of the love-phenomenon as suggested by the sounds of the words* amour, Liebe, love *and* amore, *and concludes:*

'But now imagine a people for whom love was *flucuthukh*. What can have been the particular symptoms of the general amorous disease to which such a name was given? One cannot guess. But at least it is fascinating to speculate' (1925 IV 5).

If at times the musings of writers are based on the concrete evidence of the monuments or on the views of scholars, at other times these are ignored, deformed, deliberately rejected (as we have just seen in Huxley), or denied outright. Every page by Lawrence exudes impatience and contempt for the scientists, those obtuse and prosaic prophaners of a poetic word they cannot understand. They are personified for us in that young German archaeologist who accompanies the writer and his friend Brewster during one stretch of their visit to Tarquinia. This is another of those unforgettable portraits; a pale face fed on Sauerkraut, *an old corduroy jacket, walking-boots, a bulky camera (today he would be carrying the inevitable Leica), academic ambitions and the arid scepticism of the sophisticate:* nicht viel Wert, *this place or that, this monument or that, mere ornamentation, they don't represent anything, there's nothing to be said ...*

«What is the meaning of this lion with the second head

and neck?» I asked the German. He shrugged his shoulders, and said: «Nothing!» It meant nothing to him, because nothing except the ABC of facts means anything to him. He is a scientist, and when he doesn't want a thing to have a meaning it is, *ipso facto,* meaningless.

Writers and scholars are here openly at war. The representatives of the two worlds - that of systematic enquiry and that of intuition - glare across at one another, their viewpoints diametrically opposed.

But who wants object-lessons about vanished races? What one wants is a contact. The Etruscans are not a theory or a thesis. If they are anything, they are an *experience.*

It would not make sense to judge this experience by the yardstick of true or false. Just as, after all, it would not make sense to point out the inaccuracies, the interpretative absurdities, the manifest and deliberate falsifications - from the point of view of the strict scientific method - to be met with in the fanciful writings from which I have picked out a few points. For an «experience» either exists or it does not: and this particular experience consists not so much in the discovery of the Etruscan as in the discovery of the writer's own mind, with his ideals, his sympathies, his passions, his rages. Etruria is a mere pretext for self-revelation: favourable terrain for the burgeoning of poetic flora as the mood of the times and the temper of the mind dictate. So in Dennis's Etruria there unfolds and finds expression a wanderer's Romanticism, cultured and inquisitive, with just a dash of humour; in Carducci's, a heroic Romanticism, nurtured on history; in Lawrence's and Huxley's, a paradoxical and astringent symbolism which, via the Atlantis myth of a lost world, attempts to embody the escapist impulse of our own restless era.

To grasp the absolute autonomy of this poetic approach is to understand the fallacy which clouds those simple minds who believed, and still believe, that they can glean notions and find their bearings or, as they say, «get genned up» on the Etruscan world by reading Lawrence or Huxley. I remember the peculiar case of a certain extremely distinguished lady, a devotee of things Etruscan, who, with touching seriousness, begged me to present to the Ministry a plan she had formulated for the introduction of the study of Etruscan into the middle school curriculum. *She had evidently taken the whimsy and paradoxes of Huxley's Cardan as gospel. Much of the amateurishness which is so rife, and which I referred to in my opening, and of the fixed prejudice of the public at large, stems from this inability to distinguish between the entertaining fictions of writers and the certainties and uncertainties of scholars, jumbling the two together in a solemnly pseudo-scientific hotchpotch.*

But I wouldn't like anyone to extract from this talk of mine the moral that the reasons of the heart and the reasons of science are absolutely irreconciliable when it comes to speculating about the ancient civilizations of the Etruscans. In truth, the Etruria of literary fantasy has afforded, and may still afford, useful insights and cues to the labours of the scholars themselves.

Lawrence's Etruscan Places *contains alongside the wildest imaginings, hints worthy of the meditation of the historian and the art critic. Naturally, the writer believes in the oriental origin of the Etruscans, because that is part of the myth of Etruria; but when, lounging on the beach at Ladispoli, he gazes at the Tyrrhenian darkening under the first shadows of dusk and turns his eyes to scan the heights of Cerveteri, he cannot help having his doubts about the instantaneous birth of a civilization imported from across the sea, lacking any bond with the land in which it was to flourish. He indulges in far-fetched speculation about remote, age-old interminglings between foreign seafarers and an already established indigenous civilization, and concludes almost tamely:*

> Etruria was not a colony, it was a slowly developed country.

His intuition contains the kernel of the theories that were to be marshalled with the full panoply of proof twenty years later by the authoritative German historian Franz Altheim in a valuable scholarly work on Etruscan origins.

Visiting the necropolis of Tarquinia and noting the level terrain, the scattered tombs, the occasional humps of collapsed barrows, Lawrence observes how different the place is from the necropolis at Cerveteri, so packed with sepulchral monuments; but he points out out that this contrast is merely one of appearances:

> probably, if excavations were fully carried out, here also we should find a regular city of the dead, with its streets and crossways. And probably each tomb had his little tumulus of piled earth, so that even above-ground there were streets of mounds with tomb entrances.

A shrewd and accurate remark which is borne out by, among other things, the recent aerial photographic survey of the Tarquinia burial area.

The spirit of Etruscan architecture, with its ethereally light, ephemeral, fanciful structures, the brightly painted dwellings, the wooden shrines festively adorned with fragile terracotta figurines - all this is evocatively captured in a few swift brush-strokes:

> So that the Etruscan cities vanished as completely as flowers. Only the tombs, the bulbs, were underground.

The vases of dark-clay bucchero:

> begin to open out like strange flowers, black flowers with all the softness and the rebellion of life against convention, or red-and-black flowers painted with amusing free, bold - designs. It is there nearly always in Etruscan things, the naturalness verging on the commonplace, but usually missing it, and often achieving an originality so free and bold, and so fresh, that we, who love convention and things 'reduced to a norm', call it a bastard art, and commonplace.
>
> It is useless to look in Etruscan things for 'uplift'. If you want uplift, go to the Greek and the Gothic. If you want mass, go to the Roman. But if you love the odd spontaneous forms that are never to be standardized, go to the Etruscans.

And further, on the sculpted urns of Volterra:

> Most curious these 'classic' subjects: so unclassic! ... The

Greek and Roman 'boiled' sort of form gives way to a raggedness of edge and a certain wildness of light and shade which promises the later Gothic, but which is still held down by the heavy mysticism from the East.

Whoever writes the as yet unwritten history of Etruscan art will have to reckon with these notations which, quite apart from the brilliant play of paradox, have a much greater critical relevance, and are much more richly stimulating, than many a weighty tome brought out by distinguished archaeologists.

There is, all in all, a love of things that brings us closer to them and helps us to understand their nature. Scholars need to have it, too. The sceptical, dried-out little German maliciously drawn by Lawrence's imagination may now have become an impeccable archaeologist or philologist, a past master in cataloguing ancient loom-weights, a specialist of world renown in the noses and ears of statues, a scathing critic of anyone who, in writing a book on ancient history or art, may by chance have overlooked a loom-weight or made imprecise reference to a nose or an ear but I cannot believe that he has become a historian in the true and full meaning of the world. Historical research is inconceivable without enthusiasm and without passion, because it is in itself an adventure and, the greater the obstacles, the less predictable the outcome, the more exciting is the quest.

Etruscan scholarship and the 'Etruscan romance' of our own times are, true enough, two quite different things. But the Etruscologist cannot be wholly oblivious to the appeal which the object of his studies exerts so widely in our culture. He should, indeed, respond to this appeal, welcome its emotional charge and not fear to be infected by enthusiasm. It is in this sense that the two divergent paths come together again and science can once more acknowledge its debt to the imagination.

Massimo Pallottino

(translated by John Gatt)

ETRUSCAN PLACES

The numbers on the margin refer to the plates.
Footnotes are by the editors.

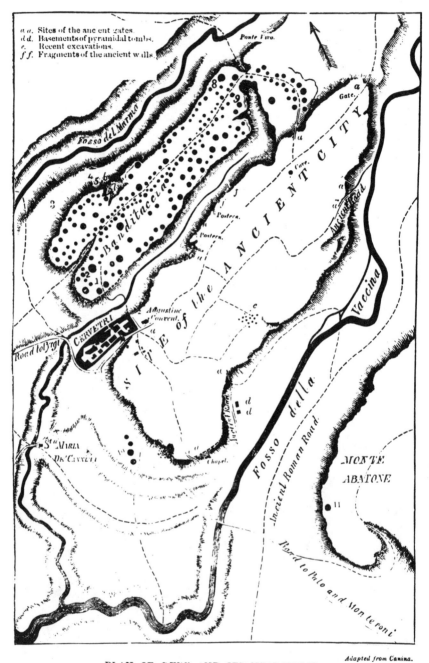

a a. Sites of the ancient gates.
d d. Basements of pyramidal tombs.
e. Recent excavations.
f f. Fragments of the ancient walls.

Ponte Faro.

Fosso del Marmo

8

9

Banditaccia

4 5 6
7

3

Cave.

ANCIENT CITY

2

1

Postera.

Postera.

Augustine Convent.

CERVETRI

Road to Brqi

e

Vaccina

Ancient Road

SITE of the

Fosso della

d
d

S.ta MARIA
DE CERVETRI

Chapel.

Ancient Roman Road.

MONTE
ABATONE

11

Road to Palo and Monteroni

Adapted from Canina.

PLAN OF CÆRE AND ITS NECROPOLIS.

1. CERVETERI

The Etruscans, as everyone knows, were the people who occupied the middle of Italy in early Roman days and whom the Romans, in their usual neighbourly fashion, wiped out entirely to make room for Rome with a very big R. They couldn't have wiped them all out, there were too many of them. But they did wiped out the Etruscan existence as a nation and a people. However, this seems to be the inevitable result of expansion with a big E, which is the sole *raison d'être* of people like the Romans.

Now, we know nothing about the Etruscans except what we find in their tombs. There are references to them in Latin writers. But of first-hand knowledge we have nothing except what the tombs offer.

So to the tombs we must go: or the museums containing the things that have been rifled from the tombs.

Myself, the first time I consciously saw Etruscan things, in the museum at Perugia, I was instinctively attracted to them. And it seems to be that way. Either there is instant sympathy, or instant contempt and indifference. Most people despise everything B.C. that isn't Greek, for the good reason that it ought to be Greek if it isn't. So Etruscan things are put down as a feeble Graeco-Roman imitation. And a great scientific historian like Mommsen hardly allows that the Etruscans existed at all. Their existence was antipathetic to him. The Prussian in him was enthralled by the Prussian in the all-conquering Romans. So being a great scientific historian, he almost denies the very existence of the Etruscan people. He didn't like the idea of them.

That was enough for a great scientific historian.

Besides, the Etruscan were vicious. We know it, because their enemies and exterminators said so. Just as we knew the unspeakable depths of *our* enemies in the late war. Who isn't vicious to his enemy? To my detractors I am a very effigy of vice. *À la bonne heure!*

However, those pure, clean-living, sweet-souled Romans, who smashed nation after nation and crushed the free soul in people after people, and were ruled by Messalina and Heliogabalus and such-like snowdrops, they said the Etruscan were vicious. So *basta! Quand le maître parle, tout le monde se tait.* The Etruscans were vicious! The only vicious people on the face of the earth presumably. You and I, dear reader, we are two unsullied snowflakes, aren't we? We have every right to judge.

Myself, however, if the Etruscans were vicious, I'm glad they were. To the Puritan all things are impure, as somebody says. And those naughty neighbours of the Romans at least escaped being Puritans.

But to the tombs, to the tombs! On a sunny April morning we set out for the tombs. From Rome, the eternal city, now in a black bonnet. It was not far to go - about twenty miles over the Campagna towards the sea, on the line to Pisa.

The Campagna, with its great green spread of growing wheat, is almost human again. But still there are damp empty tracts, where now the narcissus stands in clumps, or covers whole fields. And there are places green and foam-white, all with camomile, on a sunny morning in early April.

We are going to Cerveteri, which is the ancient Caere, or Cere, and which had a Greek nàme too, Agylla. It was a gay and gaudy Etruscan city when Rome put up her first few hovels: probably. Anyhow, there are tombs there now.

The inestimable big Italian railway-guide says the station is Palo, and Cerveteri is eight and a half kilometres away: about five miles. But there is a post-omnibus.

We arrive at Palo, a station in nowhere, and ask if there is a bus to Cerveteri. No! An ancient sort of wagon with an ancient white horse stands outside. Where does that go? To Ladispoli. We know we don't want to go to Ladispoli, so we stare at the

1. The maremma *in the neighbourhood of the necropolis at Cerveteri in the Twenties. In the background is a herdsman's hut and the outline of the Ceriti hills.*

2. *Looking north towards Cerveteri from the Fosso del Manganello.*

3. *The Banditaccia necropolis, excavated by R. Mengarelli in 1911. The Maroi tumulus - 6th to 7th centuries B.C. - containing three tombs.*

4. *The forecourt of the Maroi tumulus. Beyond is a later particoloured tumulus with bands of tufa and* macco *(5th century B.C.).*

5. *Tumulus II. In use from the mid 6th to the late 5th century B.C.. It contains four disparate tombs. 'Phallic' cippi can be seen in the foreground.*

6. Tumulus II viewed from the west in a more recent photograph.

7. Tomb 9, 'of the Greek vases', within Tumulus II. In use from the mid 6th to the late 5th century B.C.. The bed with the two triangular bed-ends is for the laying out of female dead.

8. The tomb of the Tarquins, lower chamber. In use from the early 3rd until the latter half of the 2nd century B.C., over about eight generations. There are inscriptions in Etruscan and Latin, and traces of paintings.

9. *Tomb of the Reliefs, of the Matuna family. Built around the mid 4th century B.C.*

10. *Male 'pillar' and 'phallic'* cippi, *in use from the 4th to the 3rd century B.C..*

11. *'Cottage-shaped' female* cippi.

12. *The Sorbo necropolis. The Regolini-Galassi tomb, discovered intact in 1836. First half of the 7th century B.C.*

13. The Maremma coast. Butteri - *mounted herdsmen - at the mouth of the Marta. Early 20th century.*

14. *Corneto-Tarquinia. Barriera San Giusto in the Twenties.*

15. *The Vitelleschi palace, which since 1924 has housed Tarquinia's National Museum.*

16. *Sarcophagus of the Magistrate or of Laris Pulena. 3rd-2nd century B.C.. (Tarquinia, Museo Nazionale).*

17. *Tarquinia. The Monterozzi necropolis, before the construction of the masonry entrances.*

18. *The Hunting and Fishing Tomb, discovered in 1873. Dated at 530 B.C. Complete rear wall: hunting and fishing scenes, and tympanum with banqueting scene.*

19. *The Hunting and Fishing Tomb. Detail from the left-hand wall, showing a diver.*

20. *Tombs of the Leopards, found in 1875. 475-450 B.C. Far right-hand corner: banqueting scene with dancers.*

landscape. Could we get a carriage of any sort? It would be difficult. That is what they always say: difficult! Meaning impossible. At least they won't lift a finger to help. Is there an hotel at Cerveteri? They don't know. They have none of them ever been, though it is only five miles away, and there are tombs. Well, we will leave our two bags at the station. But they cannot accept them. Because they are not locked. But when did a hold-all ever lock? Difficult! Well then, let us leave them, and steal if you want to. Impossible! Such a moral responsibility! Impossible to leave an unlocked small hold-all at the station. So much for the officials!

However, we try the man at the small buffet. He is very laconic, but seems all right. We abandon our things in a corner of the dark little eating-place, and set off on foot. Luckily it is only something after ten in the morning.

A flat, white road with a rather noble avenue of umbrella-pines for the first few hundred yards. A road not far from the sea, a bare, flattish, hot white road with nothing but a tilted oxen-wagon in the distance like a huge snail with four horns. Beside the road the tall asphodel is letting off its spasmodic pink sparks, rather at random, and smelling of cats. Away to the left is the sea, beyond the flat green wheat, the Mediterranean glistening flat and deadish, as it does on the low shores. Ahead are hills, and a ragged bit of a grey village with an ugly big grey building: that is Cerveteri. We trudge on along the dull road. After all, it is only five miles and a bit.

We creep nearer, and climb the ascent. Caere, like most Etruscan cities, lay on the crown of a hill with cliff-like escarpments. Not that this Cerveteri is an Etruscan city. Caere, the Etruscan city, was swallowed by the Romans, and after the fall of the Roman Empire it fell out of existence altogether. But it feebly revived, and today we come to an old Italian village, walled in with grey walls, and having a few new, pink, box-shaped houses and villas outside the walls.

We pass through the gateway, where men are lounging talking and mules are tied up, and in bits of crooked grey streets look for a place where we can eat. We see the notice, *Vini e Cucina*, Wines and Kitchen; but it is only a deep cavern where mule-drivers are drinking blackish wine.

However, we ask the man who is cleaning the post-omnibus in the street if there is any other place. He says no, so in we go, into the cavern, down a few steps.

Everybody is perfectly friendly. But the food is as usual, meat broth, very weak, with thin macaroni in it: the boiled meat that made the broth: and tripe: also spinach. The broth tastes of nothing, the meat tastes almost of less, the spinach, alas! has been cooked over in the fat skimmed from the boiled beef. It is a meal - with a piece of so-called sheep's cheese, that is pure salt and rancidity, and probably comes from Sardinia; and wine that tastes like, and probably is, the black wine of Calabria wetted with a good proportion of water. But it is a meal. We will go to the tombs.

Into the cavern swaggers a spurred shepherd wearing goat-skin trousers with the long, rusty brown goat's hair hanging shaggy from his legs. He grins and drinks wine, and immediately one sees again the shaggy-legged faun. His face is a faun-face, not deadened by morals. He grins quietly, and talks very subduedly, shyly, to the fellow who draws the wine from the barrels. It is obvious fauns are shy, very shy, especially of moderns like ourselves. He glances at us from a corner of his eye, ducks, wipes his mouth on the back of his hand, and is gone, clambering with his hairy legs on to his lean pony, swirling, and rattling away with a neat little clatter of hoofs, under the ramparts and away to the open. He is the faun escaping again out of the city precincts, far more shy and evanescent than any Christian virgin. You cannot hard-boil him.

It occurs to me how rarely one sees the faun-face now, in Italy, that one used to see so often before the war: the brown, rather still, straight-nosed face with a little black moustache and often a little tuft of black beard, yellow eyes, rather shy under long lashes, but able to glare with a queer glare, on occasion; and mobile lips that had a queer way of showing the teeth when talking, bright white teeth. It was an old, old type, and rather common in the South. But now you will hardly see one of these men left, with the unconscious, ungrimacing faun-face. They were all, apparently, killed in the war: they would be sure not to

survive such a war. Anyway the last one I know, a handsome
fellow of my own age - forty and a bit - is going queer and
morose, crushed between war memories, that have revived, and
remorseless go-ahead women-folk. Probably when I go South
again he will have disappeared. They can't survive, the faun-
faced men, with their pure outlines and their strange non-moral
calm. Only the deflowered faces survive.

So much for a Maremma shepherd! We went out into the
sunny April street of this Cerveteri, *Caerevetus*, the old Caere. It
is a worn-out little knot of streets shut in inside a wall. Rising on
the left is the citadel, the acropolis, the high place, that which is
the arx in Etruscan cities. But now the high place is forlorn, with
a big, weary building like a governor's palace, or a bishop's
palace[1], spreading on the crest behind the castle gate, and a
desolate sort of yard tilting below it, surrounded by ragged,
ruinous enclosure. It is forlorn beyond words, dead, and still too
big for the grey knot of inhabited streets below.

The girl of the cavern, a nice girl but a bad cook, has found
us a guide, obviously her brother, to take us to the necropolis.
He is a lad of about fourteen, and like everybody in this
abandoned place shy and suspicious, holding off. He bids us
wait while he runs away somewhere. So we drink coffee in the
tiny café outside which the motor-omnibus reposes all day long,
till the return of our guide and another little boy, who will come
with him and see him through. The two boys cotton together,
make a little word secure from us, and move on ahead of us,
ignoring us as far as possible. The stranger is always a menace.
Brewster and I are two very quiet-mannered harmless men. But
that first boy could not have borne to go alone with us. Not
alone! He would have been afraid, as if he were in the dark.

They led us out of the only gate of the old town. Mules and
ponies were tied up in the sloping, forlorn place outside, and
pack mules arrived, as in Mexico. We turned away to the left,
under the rock cliff from whose summit the so-called palace goes
up flush, the windows looking out on to the world. It seems as if
the Etruscans may once have cut this low rock-face, and as if the

---

[1] It was instead a huge medieval barn, locally known as the *granarone*.

whole crown on which the wall-girt village of Cerveteri now
stands may once have been the arx, the ark, the inner citadel and
holy place of the city of Caere, or Agylla, the splendid Etruscan
city, with its Greek quarters. There was a whole suburb of Greek
colonists, from Ionia, or perhaps from Athens, in busy Caere
when Rome was still a rather crude place. About the year 390
B.C. the Gauls came swooping down on Rome. Then the
Romans hurried the Vestal Virgins and other women and
children away to Caere, and the Etruscans took care of them, in
their rich city[2]. Perhaps the refugee Vestals were housed on this
rock. And perhaps not. The site of Caere may have not been
exactly here. Certainly it stretched away on this same hilltop, east
and south, occupying the whole of the small plateau, some four
or five miles round, and spreading a great city thirty times as big
as the present Cerveteri. But the Etruscans built everything of
wood - houses, temples - all save walls for fortification, great
gates, bridges, and drainage works. So that the Etruscan cities
vanished as completely as flowers. Only the tombs, the bulbs,
were underground. But the Etruscans built their cities, whenever
possible, on a long narrow plateau or headland above surrounding country, and they liked to have a rocky cliff for their base,
as in Cerveteri. Round the summit of this cliff, this headland,
went the enclosure wall, sometimes miles of the great cincture.
And within the walls they liked to have one inner high place, the
arx, the citadel. Then outside they liked to have a sharp dip or
ravine, with a parallel hill opposite. And on the parallel hill
opposite they liked to have their city of the dead, the necropolis.
So they could stand on their ramparts and look over the hollow
where the stream flowed among its bushes, across from the city
of life, gay with its painted houses and temples, to the near-at-
hand city of their dear dead, pleasant with its smooth walks and
stone symbols, and painted fronts.

So it is at Cerveteri. From the sea-plain - and the sea was
probably a mile or two miles nearer in, in Etruscan days - the
land leaves the coast in an easy slope to the low-crowned cliffs of
the city. But behind, turning out of the gate away from the sea,

[2] Livy V; 40

you pass under the low but sheer cliff of the town, down the stony road to the little ravine, full of bushes.

Down here in the gully, the town - village, rather - has built its wash-house[3], and the women are quietly washing the linen. They are good-looking women, of the old world, with that very attractive look of noiselessness and inwardness, which women must have had in the past. As if, within the woman, there were again something to seek, that the eye can never search out. Something that can be lost, but can never be found out.

Up the other side of the ravine is a steep, rocky little climb along a sharp path, the two lads scrambling subduedly ahead. We pass a door cut in the rock-face. I peep in to the damp, dark cell of what was apparently once a tomb. But this must have been for unimportant people, a little room in a cliff-face, now all deserted. The great tombs in the Banditaccia are covered with mounds, tumuli. No one looks at these damp little rooms in the low cliff-face, among the bushes. So I scramble on hastily, after the others.

To emerge on to the open, rough, uncultivated plain. It was like Mexico, on a small scale: the open, abandoned plain; in the distance little, pyramid-shaped mountains set down straight upon the level, in the not-far distance; and between, a mounted shepherd galloping round a flock of mixed sheep and goats, looking very small. It was just like Mexico, only much smaller and more human.

The boys went ahead across the fallow land, where there were many flowers, tiny purple verbena, tiny forget-me-nots, and much wild mignonette, that had a sweet little scent. I asked the boys what they called it. They gave the usual dumb-bell answer: «It is a flower!» On the heaping banks towards the edge of the ravine the asphodel grew wild and thick, with tall flowers up to my shoulder, pink and rather spasmodic. These asphodels are very noticeable, a great feature in all this coast landscape. I thought the boys surely would have a name for it. But no!

---

[3] The old way of access to the necropolis, the *via del Lavatore* , as it were, used to run from the Eastern wall of the medieval village. From the wash-house or *lavatore* it crossed the creek of Manganello and climbed the broad promontory of the Banditaccia. Today, the common way of access follows a different path, to the West of the village.

Sheepishly they make the same answer: «*E' un fiore! Puzza!*» - It
is a flower. It stinks! - Both facts being self-evident, there was no
contradicting it. Though the smell of the asphodel is not
objectionable, to me: and I find the flower, now I know it well,
very beautiful, with its way of opening some pale, big, starry
pink flowers, and leaving many of its buds shut, with their dark,
reddish stripes.

Many people, however, are very disappointed with the
Greeks, for having made so much of this flower. It is true, the
word «asphodel» makes one expect some tall and mysterious
lily, not this sparky, assertive flower with just a touch of the
onion about it. But for me, I don't care for mysterious lilies, not
even for that weird shyness the mariposa lily has. And having
stood on the rocks in Sicily, with the pink asphodel proudly
sticking up like clouds at sea, taller than myself, letting off pink
different flowerets with such sharp and vivid *éclat* , and saving
up such a store of buds in ear, stripey, I confess I admire the
flower. It has a certain reckless glory, such as the Greeks loved.

One man said he thought we were mistaken in calling this
the Greek asphodel, as somewhere in Greek the asphodel is
called yellow. Therefore, said this scholastic Englishman, the
asphodel of the Greeks was probably the single daffodil.

But not it! There is a very nice and silky yellow asphodel on
Etna, pure gold. And heaven knows how common the wild
daffodil is in Greece. It does not seem a very Mediterranean
flower. The narcissus, the polyanthus narcissus, is pure Mediterranean, and Greek. But the daffodil, the Lent lily!

However, trust an Englishman and a modern for wanting to
turn the tall, proud, sparky, dare-devil asphodel into the modest
daffodil! I believe we don't like the asphodel because we don't
like anything proud and sparky. The myrtle opens her blossoms
in just the same way as the asphodel, explosively, throwing
out the sparks of her stamens. And I believe it was just that the
Greeks *saw*. They were that way themselves.

However, this is all on the way to the tombs: which lie
ahead, mushroom-shaped mounds of grass, great mushroom-
shaped mounds, along the edge of the ravine. When I say ravine,
don't expect a sort of Grand Canyon. Just a modest, Italian sort

of ravine-gully, that you could almost jump down.

When we come near we see the mounds have bases of stone 3
masonry, great girdles of carved and bevelled stone, running
round touching the earth in flexible, uneven lines, like the girdles
on big, uneasy buoys half sunk in the sea. And they are sunk a
bit in the ground. And there is an avenue of mounds, with a 6
sunken path between, parallel to the ravine. This was evidently
the grand avenue of the necropolis, like the million-dollar
cemetery in New Orleans. *Absit omen!*

Between us and the mounds is a barbed-wire fence. There is
a wire gate on which it says you mustn't pick the flowers,
whatever that may mean, for there are no flowers. And another
notice says, you mustn't tip the guide, as he is gratuitous.

The boys run to the new little concrete house just by, and
bring the guide: a youth with red eyes and a bandaged hand. He
lost a finger on the railway a month ago. He is shy, and
muttering, and neither prepossessing nor cheerful, but he turns
out quite decent. He brings keys and a acetylene lamp, and we
go through the wire gate into the place of tombs.

There is a queer stillness and a curious peaceful repose about
the Etruscan places I have been to, quite different from the
weirdness of Celtic places, the slightly repellent feeling of Rome
and the old Campagna, and the rather horrible feeling of the
great pyramid places in Mexico, Teotihuacan and Cholula, and
Mitla in the south; or the amiably idolatrous Buddha places in
Ceylon[4]. There is a stillness and a softness in these great grassy
mounds with their ancient stone girdles, and down the central
walk there lingers still a kind of homeliness and happiness. True,
it was a still and sunny afternoon in April, and larks rose from
the soft grass of the tombs. But there was a stillness and a
soothingness in all the air, in that sunken place, and a feeling
that it was good for one's soul to be there.

The same when we went down the few steps, and into the 7
chambers of rock, within the tumulus. There is nothing left. It is
like a house that has been swept bare: the inmates have left: now

---

[4] L. had visited Ceylon in 1922, where he had stayed at the Brewsters'. Later in the
same year, he had gone to Mexico.

it waits for the next comer. But whoever it is that has departed,
they have left a pleasant feeling behind them, warm to the heart,
and kindly to the bowels.

They are surprisingly big and handsome, these homes of the
dead. Cut out of the living rock, they are just like houses. The
roof has a beam cut to imitate the roof-beam of the house. It is a
house, a home.

As you enter, there are two small chambers, one to the right,
one to the left, antechambers. They say that here the ashes of the
slaves were deposited, in urns, upon the great benches of rock.
For the slaves were always burned, presumably. Whereas at
Cerveteri the masters were laid full-length, sometimes in the
great stone sarcophagi, sometimes in big coffins of terra-cotta, in
all their regalia. But most often they were just laid there on the
broad rock-bed that goes round the tomb, and is empty now,
laid there calmly upon an open bier, not shut in sarcophagi, but
sleeping as if in life.

The central chamber is large; perhaps there is a great square
column of rock left in the centre, apparently supporting the solid
roof as a roof-tree supports the roof of a house. And all round
the chamber goes the broad bed of rock, sometimes a double
tier, on which the dead where laid, in their coffins, or lying open
upon carved litters of stone or wood, a man glittering in golden
armour, or a woman in white and crimson robes, with great
necklaces round their necks, and rings on their fingers. Here lay
the family, the great chiefs and their wives, the Lucumones, and
their sons and daughters, many in one tomb.

Beyond again is a rock doorway, rather narrow, and
narrowing upwards, like Egypt. The whole thing suggests Egypt:
but on the whole, here all is plain, simple, usually with no
decoration, and with those easy natural proportions whose
beauty one hardly notices, they come so naturally, physically. It
is the natural beauty of proportion of the phallic consciousness,
contrasted with the more studied or ecstatic proportion of the
mental and spiritual consciousness we are accustomed to.

Through the inner doorway is the last chamber, small and
dark and culminative. Facing the door goes the stone bed on
which was laid, presumably, the Lucumo and the sacred

treasures of the dead, the little bronze ship of death that should bear him over to the other world, the vases of jewels for his arraying, the vases of small dishes, the little bronze statuettes and tools, the weapons, the armour: all the amazing impedimenta of the important dead. Or sometimes in this inner room lay the woman, the great lady, in all her robes, with the mirror in her hand, and her treasures, her jewels and combs and silver boxes of cosmetics, in urns or vases ranged along-side. Splendid was the array they went with, into death.

One of the most important tombs is the *tomb of the Tarquins*, the family that gave Etruscan kings to early Rome. 8 You go down a flight of steps, and into the underworld home of the Tarchne, as the Etruscans wrote it. In the middle of the great chamber there are two pillars, left from the rock. The walls of the big living-room of the dead Tarquins, if one may put it so, are stuccoed, but there are no paintings. Only there are the writings on the wall, and in the burial niches in the wall above the long double-tier stone bed; little sentences freely written in red paint or black, or scratched in the stucco with the finger, slanting with the real Etruscan carelessness and fullness of life, often running downwards, written from right to left. We can read these debonair inscriptions, that look as if someone had just chalked them up yesterday without a thought, in the archaic Etruscan letters, quite easily. But when we have read them we don't know what they mean. *Avle tarchnas larthal clan.* That is plain enough. But what does it mean? Nobody knows precisely. Names, family names, family connections, titles of the dead - we may assume so much. «Aule, son of Larte Tarchna», say the scientists, having got so far. But we cannot read one single sentence. The Etruscan language is a mystery. Yet in Caesar's day it was the everyday language of the bulk of the people in central Italy - at least, west-central. And many Romans spoke Etruscan as we speak French. Yet now the language is entirely lost. Destiny is a queer thing.

The tomb called the *Grotta Bella,* or *tomb of the Reliefs* is 9 interesting of the low-relief carvings and stucco reliefs on the pillars and the walls round the burial niches and above the stone death-bed that goes around the tomb. The things represented are mostly warriors' arms and insignia: shields, helmets, corselets, greaves for the legs, swords, spears, shoes, belts, the necklace of the noble: and then the sacred drinking bowl, the sceptre, the dog who is man's guardian even on the death journey, the two lions that stand by the gateway of life or death, the triton, or merman, and the goose, the bird that swims on the waters and thrusts its head deep into the flood of the Beginning and the End. All these are represented on the walls. And all these, no doubt, were laid, the actual objects, or figures to represent them, in this tomb. But now nothing is left. But when we remember the great store of treasure that every notable tomb must have contained: and that every large tumulus covered several tombs: and that in the necropolis of Cerveteri we can still discover hundreds of tombs: and that other tombs exist in great numbers on the other side of the old city, towards the sea; we can have an idea of the vast mass of wealth this city could afford to bury with its dead, in days when Rome had very little gold, and even bronze was precious.

The tombs seem so easy and friendly, cut out of rock underground. One does not feel oppressed, descending into them. It must be partly owing to the peculiar charm of natural proportion which is in all Etruscan things of the unspoilt, unromanized centuries. There is a simplicity, combined with a most peculiar, free-breasted naturalness and spontaneity, in the shapes and movements of the underworld walls and spaces, that at once reassures the spirit. The Greeks sought to make an impression, and Gothic still more seeks to impress the mind. The Etruscans, no. The things they did, in their easy centuries, are as natural and as easy as breathing. They leave the breast breathing freely and pleasantly, with a certain fullness of life. Even the tombs. And that is the true Etruscan quality: ease, naturalness, and an abundance of life, no need to force the mind or the soul in any direction.

And death, to the Etruscan, was a pleasant continuance of life, with jewels and wine and flutes playing for the dance. It was neither an ecstasy of bliss, a heaven, nor a purgatory of torment. It was just a natural continuance of the fullness of life. Everything was in terms of life, of living.

Yet everything Etruscan, save the tomb, has been wiped out. It seems strange. One goes out again into the April sunshine, into the sunken road between the soft, grassy-mounded tombs, and as one passes one glances down the steps at the doorless doorways of tombs. It is so still and pleasant and cheerful. The place is so soothing.

Brewster, who has just come back from India, is so surprised to see the phallic stones by the doors of many tombs. Why, it's 5 like the Shiva *lingams*[5] at Benares. It's exactly like the lingam stones in the Shiva caves and the Shiva temples!

And that is another curious thing. One can live one's life, and read all the books about India or Etruria, and never read a single word about the thing that impresses one in the very first five minutes, in Benares or in an Etruscan necropolis: that is, the phallic symbol. Here it is, in stone, unmistakable, and everywhere around these tombs. Here it is, big and little, standing by the doors, or inserted, quite small, into the rock: the phallic stone! Perhaps some tumuli had a great phallic column on the summit: some perhaps by the door. There are still small phallic stones, only seven or eight inches long, inserted in the rock outside the doors: they always seem to have been outside. 10 And these small lingams look as if they were part of the rock. But no, Brewster lifts one out. It is cut, and it is fitted into a socket, previously cemented in. Brewster puts the phallic stone back into its socket, where it was placed, probably, five or six hundred years before Christ was born. The big phallic stones that, it is said, probably stood on top of the tumuli, are sometimes carved very beautifully, sometimes with inscriptions. The scientists call them *cippus, cippi*. But surely the cippus is a truncated column used usually as a gravestone: a column quite squat, often square, having been cut across, truncated, to represent maybe a life cut short. Some of the little phallic stones are like this - truncated. But others are tall, huge and decorated, and with the double cone that is surely phallic. And the little inserted phallic stones are not cut short.

---

[5] *Lingam* and *yoni* are in Sanskrit the symbols of the male and female sex, frequently represented in sculpture and endowed of some sacred significance.

By the doorway of some tombs there is a carved stone house, or a stone imitation chest with sloping lids like the two sides of the roof on an oblong house. The guide-boy, who works on the railway and is no profound scholar, mutters that every woman's tomb had one of these stone houses or chests over it - over the doorway, he says - and every man's tomb had one of the phallic stones, or lingams. But since the great tombs were family tombs, perhaps they had both.

The stone house, as the boy calls it, suggests the Noah's Ark without the boat part: the Noah's Ark box we had as children, full of animals. And that is what it is, the Ark, the *arx*, the womb. The womb of all the world, that brought forth all the creatures. The womb, the *arx*, where life retreats in the last refuge. The womb, the ark of the covenant, in which lies the mystery of eternal life, the manna and the mysteries. There it is, standing displaced outside the doorway of Etruscan tombs at Cerveteri.

And perhaps in the insistence on these two symbols, in the Etruscan world, we can see the reason for the utter destruction and the annihilation of the Etruscan consciousness. The new world wanted to rid itself of these fatal, dominant symbols of the old world, the old physical world. The Etruscan consciousness was rooted quite blithely in these symbols, the phallus and the arx. So the whole consciousness, the whole Etruscan pulse and rhythm, must be wiped out.

Now we see again, under the blue heavens where the larks are singing in the hot April sky, why the Romans called the Etruscans vicious. Even in their palmy days the Romans were not exactly saints. But they thought they ought to be. They hated the phallus and the ark, because they wanted empire and dominion and, above all, riches: social gain. You cannot dance gaily to the double flute and at the same time conquer nations or rake in large sums of money. *Delenda est Carthago*. To the greedy man, everybody that is in the way of its greed is vice incarnate.

There are many tombs, though not many of the great mounds are left. Most have been levelled. There are many tombs: some were standing half full of water; some were in the process of being excavated, in a kind of quarry-place, though the work for the time was silent and abandoned. Many tombs, many, many, and you must descend to them all, for they are all cut below the surface of the earth: and where there was a tumulus it was piled above them afterwards, loose earth, within the girdle of stone. Some tumuli have been levelled, yet the whole landscape is lumpy with them. But the tombs remain, here all more or less alike, though some are big and some are small, and some are noble and some are rather mean. But most of them seem to have several chambers, beyond the antechambers. And all these tombs along the dead highway would seem to have been topped, once, by the beautiful roundness of tumuli, the great mounds of fruition, for the dead, with the tall phallic cone rising from the summit.

The necropolis, as far as we are concerned, ends on a waste place of deserted excavation and flood-water. We turn back, to leave the home of dead Etruscans. All the tombs are empty. All have been rifled. The Romans may have respected the dead, for a certain time, while their religion was sufficiently Etruscan to *1* exert a power over them. But later, when the Romans started collecting Etruscan antiques - as we collect antiques today - there must have been a great sacking of the tombs. Even when all the gold and silver and jewels had been pilfered from the urns - which no doubt happened very soon after the Roman dominion - still the vases and the bronze must have remained in their places. Then the rich Romans began to collect vases, «Greek» vases with the painted scenes. So these were stolen from the tombs. Then the little bronze figures, statuettes, animals, bronze ships, of which the Etruscans put thousands in the tombs, became the rage with the Roman collectors. Some smart Roman gentry would have a thousand or two choice little Etruscan bronzes to boast of. Then Rome fell, and the barbarians pillaged whatever was left. So it went on.

And still some tombs remained virgin, for the earth had washed in and filled the entrance way, covered the stone bases of the mounds; trees, bushes grew over the graves; you had only hilly, humpy, bushy waste country.

Under these tombs lay silent, either ravaged, or, in a few

wonderful cases, still virgin. And still absolutely virgin lay one of
the tombs of Cerveteri, alone and apart from the necropolis,
buried on the other side of the town, until 1836, when it was
discovered: and, of course, denuded. General Galassi and arch-
priest Regolini unearthed it: so it is called the *Regolini-Galassi*
tomb.

12

It is still interesting: a primitive narrow tomb like a passage,
with a partition half-way, and covered with an arched roof,
what they call the false arch, which is made by letting the flat
horizontal stones of the roof jut out step by step, as they pile
upwards, till they almost meet. Then big flat stones are laid as
cover, and make the flat top of the almost Gothic arch: an arch
built, probably, in the eighth century before Christ.

In the first chamber lay the remains of a warrior, with his
bronze armour, beautiful and sensitive as if it had grown in life
for the living body, sunk on his dust. In the inner chamber
beautiful, frail, pale-gold jewellery lay on the stone bed, earrings
where the ears were dust, bracelets in the dust that once was
arms, surely of a noble lady, nearly three thousand years ago.

They took away everything. The treasure, so delicate and
sensitive and wistful, is mostly in the Gregorian Museum in the
Vatican. On two of the little silver vases from the Regolini-
Galassi tomb is the scratched inscription - *MI LARTHIA*.
Almost the first written Etruscan words we know. And what do
they mean, anyhow? «This is Larthia» - Larthia being a lady ?

Caere, even seven hundred years before Christ, must have
been rich and full of luxury, fond of soft gold and of banquets,
dancing, and great Greek vases. But you will find none of it
now. The tombs are bare: what treasure they yielded up, and
even to us Cerveteri has yielded a great deal, is in the museums.
If you go you will see, as I saw, a grey, forlorn little township in
tight walls - perhaps having a thousand inhabitants - and some
empty burying places.

But when you sit in the post-automobile, to be rattled down
to the station, about four o' clock in the sunny afternoon, you
will probably see the bus surrounded by a dozen buxom,
handsome women, saying good-bye to one of their citizenesses.
And in the full, dark, handsome, jovial faces surely you see the

lustre still of the life-loving Etruscans! They are some level Greek eyebrows. But surely there are other vivid, warm faces still jovial with Etruscan vitality, beautiful with the mystery of the unrifled ark, ripe with the phallic knowledge and the Etruscan carelessness!

MAP OF TARQUINII AND ITS NECROPOLIS. (ADAPTED FROM WESTPHAL.)

TAROVINII

La Carolina.

La Civita.

IL MONTA ROZZI.

NECROPOLIS

FIVME MARTA

CORNETO.

Road to Tuscanella.

Road to Montalto.

Road to Civita Vecchia.

and Vulci.

Road to Corneto.

Road to Toscanella.

1 Roman mile.

a Grotta Querciola.
b Grotta del Triclinio, and G. del Morto.
c Grotta de' Pompej.
d Grotta del Cardinale.

e Grotta delle Bighe, G. del Mare.
   G. del Barone G. Francesca, and
   G. della Scrofa Nera.
f Grotta delle Iscrizioni.
g La Mercareccia.

h Caves.
i Sites of the ancient gates.
k Fragments of the ancient walls.
l Ara della Regina, or the Acropolis.
m Aqueduct.

=== Carriage-roads.
——— Carriage-roads or bridle-paths.
—— Country-roads or ancient roads.
- - - Lines of ancient roads. Where it connects the portions of m it marks the subterranean course of the aqueduct.

2. TARQUINIA

In Cerveteri there is nowhere to sleep, so the only thing to do is to go back to Rome, or forwards to Civitavecchia. The bus landed us at the station of Palo at about five o'clock: in the midst of nowhere: to meet the Rome train. But we were going on to Tarquinia, not back to Rome, so we must wait two hours, till seven.

In the distance we could see the concrete villas and new houses of what was evidently Ladispoli, a seaside place, some two miles away. So we set off to walk to Ladispoli, on the flat sea-road. On the left, in the wood that forms part of the great park, the nightingales had already begun to whistle, and looking over the wall one could see many little rose-coloured cyclamens glowing on the earth in the evening light.

We walked on, and the Rome train came surging round the bend. It misses Ladispoli, whose two miles of branch line runs only in the hot bathing months. As we neared the first ugly villas on the road the ancient wagonette drawn by the ancient white horse, both looking sun-bitten almost to ghostliness, clattered past. It just beat us.

Ladispoli is one of those ugly little places on the Roman coast, consisting of new concrete villas, new concrete hotels, kiosks and bathing establishments; bareness and non-existence for ten months in the year, seething solid with fleshy bathers in July and August. Now it was deserted, quite deserted, save for two or three officials and four wild children.

Brewster and I lay on the grey-black lava sand, by the flat, low sea, over which the sky, grey and shapeless, emitted a flat, wan evening light. Little waves curled green out of the sea's dark greyness, from the curious low flatness of the water. It is a peculiarly forlorn coast, the sea peculiarly flat and sunken, lifeless-looking, the land as if it had given its last gasp, and was now for ever inert.

13   Yet this is the Tyrrhenian sea of the Etruscans, where their shipping spread sharp sails, and beat the sea with slave-oars, roving in from Greece and Sicily, Sicily of the Greek tyrants; from Cumae, the city of the old Greek colony of Campania, where the province of Naples now is; and from Elba, where the Etruscans mined their iron ore. The Etruscans sailed the seas. They are even said to have come by sea, from Lydia in Asia Minor, at some date far back in the dim mists before the eight century B.C. But that a whole people, even a whole host, sailed in the tiny ships of those days, all at once, to people a sparsely peopled central Italy, seems hard to imagine. Probably ships did come - even before Ulysses. Probably men landed on the strange flat coast, and made camps, and then treated with the natives. Whether the newcomers were Lydians or Hittites with hair curled in a roll behind, or men from Mycenae or Crete, who knows. Perhaps men of all these sorts came, in batches. For in Homeric days a restlessness seems to have possessed the Mediterranean basin, and ancient races began shaking ships like seeds over the sea. More people than Greeks, or Hellenes, or Indo-Germanic groups, were on the move.

But whatever little ships were run ashore on the soft, deep, grey-black volcanic sand of this coast, three thousand years ago, and earlier, their mariners certainly did not find those hills inland empty of people. If the Lydians or Hittites pulled up their long little two-eyed ships on to the beach, and made a camp behind a bank, in shelter from the wet strong wind, what natives came down curiously to look at them? For natives there were, of that we may be certain. Even before the fall of Troy, before even Athens was dreamed of, there were natives here. And they had huts on the hills, thatched huts in clumsy groups most probably; with patches of grain, and flocks of goats and probably cattle.

Probably it was like coming on an old Irish village, or a village in the Scottish Hebrides in Prince Charlie's day, to come upon a village of these Italian aborigines, by the Tyrrhenian sea, three thousand years ago. But by the time Etruscan history starts in Caere, some eight centuries B.C., there was certainly more than a village on the hill. There was a native city, of that we may be sure; and a busy spinning of linen and beating of gold, long before the Regolini-Galassi tomb was built.

However that may be, somebody came, and somebody was already here: of that we may be certain and, in the first place, none of them were Greeks or Hellenes. It was the days before Rome rose up: probably when the first comers arrived it was the days even before Homer. The newcomers, whether they were few or many, seem to have come from the east, Asia Minor or Crete or Cyprus. They were, we must feel, of an old, primitive Mediterranean and Asiatic or Aegean stock. The twilight of the beginning of our history was the nightfall of some previous history, which will never be written. Pelasgian is but a shadow-word. But Hittite and Minoan, Lydian, Carian, Etruscan, these words emerge from the shadow, and perhaps from one and the same great shadow come the peoples to whom the names belong.

The Etruscan civilization seems a shoot, perhaps the last, from the prehistoric Mediterranean world, and the Etruscans, newcomers and aborigines alike, probably belonged to that ancient world, though they were of different nations and levels of culture. Later, of course, the Greeks exerted a great influence. But that is another matter.

Whatever happened, the newcomers in ancient central Italy found many natives flourishing in possession of the land. These aboriginals, now ridiculously called *Villanovans*[1], were neither wiped out nor suppressed. Probably they welcomed the strangers, whose pulse was not hostile to their own. Probably the

---

[1] In 1853, Count Giovanni Gozzadini discovered at Villanova near Bologna an archaic burial-ground from the Italian Early Iron Age. «Villanovan» is therefore the conventional term used to define the culture of that period, which is characterized by «cremation tombs with ashes placed in large black earthenware urns in the shape of a double cone decorated with incised geometrical motifs» (Pallottino 1968; 48). This culture dates from the late tenth to the late eighth century before Christ.

more highly developed religion of the newcomers was not hostile to the primitive religion of the aborigines: no doubt the two religions had the same root. Probably the aborigines formed willingly a sort of religious aristocracy from the newcomers: the Italians might almost do the same today. And so the Etruscan world arose. But it took centuries to arise. Etruria was not a colony, it was a slowly developed country.

There was never an Etruscan nation: only, in historical times, a great league of tribes or nations using the Etruscan language and the Etruscan script - at least officially - and uniting in their religious feeling and observances. The Etruscan alphabet seems to have been borrowed from the old Greeks, apparently from the Chalcidians of Cumae - the Greek colony just north of where Naples now is. But the Etruscan language is not akin to any of the Greek dialects, nor, apparently, to the Italic. But we don't know. It is probably to a great extent the language of the old aboriginals of Southern Etruria, just as the religion is in all probability basically aboriginal, belonging to some vast old religion of the prehistoric world. From the shadow of the prehistoric world emerge dying religions that have not yet invented gods or goddesses, but live by the mystery of the elemental powers in the Universe, the complex vitalities of what we feebly call Nature. And the Etruscan religion was certainly one of these. The gods and goddesses don't seem to have emerged in any sharp definiteness.

But it is not for me to make assertions. Only, that which half emerges from the dim background of time is strangely stirring; and after having read all the learned suggestions, most of them contradicting one another; and then having looked sensitively at the tombs and the Etruscan things that are left, one must accept one's own resultant feeling.

Ships came along this low, inconspicuous sea, coming up from the Near East, we should imagine, even in the days of Solomon - even, maybe, in the days of Abraham. And they kept on coming. As the light of history dawns and brightens, we see them winging along their white or scarlet sails. Then, as the Greeks came crowding into colonies in Italy, and the Phoenicians began to exploit the western Mediterranean, we begin to hear of the silent Etruscans, and to see them.

Just north of here Caere founded a port called Pyrgi, and we know that the Greek vessels flocked in, with vases and stuffs and colonists coming from Hellas or from Magna Graecia, and that Phoenician ships came rowing sharply, over from Sardinia, up from Carthage, round from Tyre and Sidon; while the Etruscans had their own fleets, built of timber from the mountains, caulked with pitch from northern Volterra, fitted with sails from Tarquinia, filled with wheat from the bountiful plains, or with the famous Etruscan articles of bronze and iron, which they carried away to Corinth or to Athens or to the ports of Asia Minor. We know of the great and finally disastrous sea-battles with the Phoenicians and the tyrant of Syracuse[2]. And we know that the Etruscans, all except those of Caere, became ruthless pirates, almost like the Moors and the Barbary corsairs later on. This was part of their viciousness, a great annoyance to their loving and harmless neighbours, the law-abiding Romans - who believed in the supreme law of conquest.

However, all this is long ago. The very coast has changed since then. The smitten sea has sunk and fallen back, the weary land has emerged when, apparently, it didn't want to, and the flowers of the coast-line are miserable bathing-places such as Ladispoli and seaside Ostia, desecration put upon desolation, to the triumphant trump of the mosquito.

The wind blew flat and almost chill from the darkening sea, the dead waves lifted small bits of pure green out of the leaden greyness, under the laden sky. We got up from the dark grey but soft sand, and went back along the road to the station, peered at by the few people and officials who were holding the place together till the next bathers came.

At the station there was general desertedness. But our things still lay untouched in a dark corner of the buffet, and the man gave us a decent meal of cold meats and wine and oranges. It

---

[2] In 474 B.C., the Syracusans defeated the Etruscans in a sea battle near Cuma. This battle, the memory of which is still marked by the Etruscan helmets offered by the victors at the Temple of Olympia, was symptomatic of the waning of Etruscan influence at sea from the fifth century B.C.(Pallottino 1968; 136).

was already night. The train came rushing in, punctually.

It is an hour or more to Civitavecchia, which is a port of not much importance, except that from here the regular steamers sail to Sardinia. We gave our things to a friendly old porter, and told him to take us to the nearest hotel. It was night, very dark as we emerged from the station.

And a fellow came furtively shouldering up to me.

«You are foreigners, aren't you?»

«Yes.»

«What nationality?»

«English.»

«You have your permission to reside in Italy - or your passport?»

«My passport I have - what do you want?»

«I want to look at your passport.»

«It's in the valise! And why? Why is this?»

«This is a port, and we must examine the papers of foreigners.»

«And why? Genoa is a port, and no one dreams of asking for papers.»

I was furious. He made no answer. I told the porter to go on to the hotel, and the fellow furtively followed at our side, half-a-pace to the rear, in the mongrel way these spy-louts have.

In the hotel I asked for a room and registered, and then the fellow asked again for my passport. I wanted to know why he demanded it, what he meant by accosting me outside the station as if I was a criminal, what he meant by insulting us with his requests, when in any other town in Italy one went unquestioned - and so forth, in considerable rage.

He did not reply, but obstinately looked as though he would be venomous if he could. He peered at the passport - though I doubt if he could make head or tail of it - asked where we were going, peered at Brewster's passport, half excused himself in a whining, disgusting sort of fashion, and disappeared into the night. A real lout.

I was furious. Supposing I had not been carrying my passport - and usually I don't dream of carrying it - what amount of trouble would the lout have made for me! Probably I should have spent the night in prison, and been bullied by half a dozen low bullies.

Those poor rats at Ladispoli had seen me and Brewster go to the sea and sit on the sand for half an hour, then go back to the train. And this was enough to rouse their suspicions, I imagine, so they telegraphed to Civitavecchia. Why are officials always fools? Even when there is no war on? What could they imagine we were doing?

The hotel manager, propitious, said there was a very interesting museum in Civitavecchia, and wouldn't we stay the next day and see it. «Ah!» I replied. «But all it contains is Roman stuff, and we don't want to look at that.» It was malice on my part, because the present regime considers itself purely ancient Roman. The man looked at me scared, and I grinned at him. «But what do they mean,» I said, «behaving like this to a simple traveller, in a country where foreigners are invited to travel!» «Ah!» said the porter softly and soothingly. «It is the Roman province. You will have no more of it when you leave the Provincia di Roma.» And when the Italians give the soft answer to turn away wrath, the wrath somehow turns away.

We walked for an hour in the dull street of Civitavecchia. There seemed so much suspicion, one would have thought there were several wars on. The hotel manager asked if we were staying. We said we were leaving by the eight-o'clock train in the morning, for Tarquinia.

And, sure enough, we left by the eight-o'clock train. Tarquinia is only one station from Civitavecchia - about twenty minutes over the flat Maremma country, with the sea on the left, and the green wheat growing luxuriantly, the asphodel sticking up its spikes.

We soon saw Tarquinia, its towers pricking up like antennae on the side of a low bluff of a hill, some few miles inland from the sea. And this was once the metropolis of Etruria, chief city of the great Etruscan League. But it died like all the other Etruscan cities, and had a more or less medieval rebirth, with a new name. Dante knew it, as it was known for centuries, as Corneto - Corgnetum or Cornetium - and forgotten was its Etruscan past. Then there was a feeble sort of wakening to remembrance a hundred years ago, and the town got Tarquinia tacked on to its Corneto: Corneto-Tarquinia[3]. The Fascist regime, however, glorying in the Italian origins of Italy, has now struck out the Corneto, so the town is once more, simply, Tarquinia. As you come up in the motor-bus from the station you see the great black letters, on a white ground, painted on the wall by the city gateway: *TARQUINIA*. So the wheel of revolution turns. There stands the Etruscan word - Latinized Etruscan - beside the medieval gate, put up by the Fascist power to name and unname.

But the Fascists, who consider themselves in all things Roman, Roman of the Caesars, heirs of Empire and world power, are beside the mark restoring the rags of dignity to Etruscan places. For all the Italian people that ever lived, the Etruscans were surely the least Roman. Just as, of all the people that ever rose up in Italy, the Romans of ancient Rome were surely the most un-Italian, judging from the natives of today.

Tarquinia is only about three miles from the sea. The omnibus soon runs one up, charges through the widened gateway, and is finished. We descend in the bare place, which seems to expect nothing. On the left is a beautiful stone palazzo - on the right is a café, upon the low ramparts above the gate. The man of the *Dazio*, the town custom, looks to see if anybody has brought food-stuffs into the town - but it is a mere glance. I ask him for the hotel. He says: «Do you mean to sleep?» I say I do. Then he tells a small boy to carry my bag and takes us to Gentile's[4].

Nowhere is far off, in these small wall-girdled cities. In the warm April morning the stony little town seems half-asleep. As a

[3] Dante mentions Corneto as the birthplace of the famous brigand Rinieri (Inferno XII, 137), and as the southern limit of the harsh Maremma scrubland to which he likened the wood of the suicides
(Inferno XIII, 9)
The wild beasts which avoid the tended land
aren't by such thorny tangled thickets bound
between where Cecina and Corneto stand.

[4] A plaque, laid on the fiftieth anniversary of L.'s visit by the «Società Tarquiniese di Arte e Storia», can now be seen in the wall of the building which houses the old Locanda Gentile, a little way from Palazzo Vitelleschi, in Via C. Battisti, formerly Via del Mare, No. 3.

matter of fact, most of the inhabitants are out in the fields, and won't come in through the gates again till evening. The slight sense of desertedness is everywhere - even in the inn, when we have climbed up the stairs to it, for the ground floor does not belong. A little lad in long trousers, who would seem to be only twelve years old but who has the air of a mature man, confronts us with his chest out. We ask for rooms. He eyes us, darts away for the key, and leads us off upstairs another flight, shouting to a young girl, who acts as chambermaid, to follow on. He shows us two small rooms, opening off a big, desert sort of general assembly room common in this kind of inn. «And you won't be lonely,» he said briskly, «because you can talk to one another through the wall. «*Toh! Lina!*» He lifts his finger and listens. «*Eh!*» comes through the wall, like an echo, with startling nearness and clearness. «*Fai presto!*» says Albertino. «*E' pronto!*» comes the voice of Lina. «*Ecco!*» says Albertino to us. «You hear!» We certainly did. The partition wall must have been butter-muslin. And Albertino was delighted, having reassured us we should not feel lonely nor frightened in the night.

He was, in fact, the most manly and fatherly little hotel manager I have ever known, and he ran the whole place. He was in reality fourteen years old, but stunted. From five in the morning till ten at night he was on the go, never ceasing, and with a queer, abrupt, sideways-darting alacrity that must have wasted a great deal of energy. The father and mother were in the background - quite young and pleasant. But they didn't seem to exert themselves. Albertino did it all. How Dickens would have loved him! But Dickens would not have seen the queer wistfulness, and courage in the boy. He was absolutely unsuspicious of us strangers. People must be rather human and decent in Tarquinia, even the commercial travellers: who, presumably, are chiefly buyers of agricultural produce, and sellers of agricultural implements and so forth.

We sallied out, back to the space by the gate, and drank coffee at one of the tin tables outside. Beyond the wall there were a few new villas - the land dropped green and quick, to the strip of coast plain and the indistinct, faintly gleaming sea, which seemed somehow not like a sea at all.

I was thinking, if this were still an Etruscan city, there would still be this cleared space just inside the gate. But instead of a rather forlorn vacant lot it would be a sacred clearing, with a little temple to keep it alert.

Myself, I like to think of the little wooden temples of the early Greeks and of the Etruscans: small, dainty, fragile, and evanescent as flowers. We have reached the stage when we are weary of huge stone erections, and we begin to realize that it is better to keep life fluid and changing than to try to hold it fast down in heavy monuments. Burdens on the face of the earth are man's ponderous erections.

The Etruscans made small temples, like little houses with pointed roofs, entirely of wood. But then, outside, they had friezes and cornices and crests of terra-cotta, so that the upper part of the temple would seem almost made of earthenware, terra-cotta plaques fitted neatly, and alive with freely modelled painted figures in relief, gay dancing creatures, rows of ducks, round faces like the sun, and faces grinning and putting out a tongue, all vivid and fresh and unimposing. The whole thing small and dainty in proportion, and fresh, somehow charming instead of impressive. There seems to have been in Etruscan instinct a real desire to preserve the natural humour of life. And that is a task surely more worthy, and even much more difficult in the long run, than conquering the world or sacrificing the self or saving the immortal soul.

Why has mankind had such a craving to be imposed upon? Why this lust after imposing creeds, imposing deeds, imposing buildings, imposing language, imposing works of art? The thing becomes an imposition and a weariness at last. Give us things that are alive and flexible, which won't last too long and become an obstruction and a weariness. Even Michelangelo becomes at last a lump and a burden and a bore. It is so hard to see past him.

Across the space from the café is the Palazzo Vitelleschi, a
15 charming building, now a national museum - so the marble slab says. But the heavy doors are shut. The place opens at ten, a man says. It is nine-thirty. We wander up the steep but not very long street, to the top.

And the top is a fragment of public garden, and a look-out. Two old men are sitting in the sun, under a tree. We walk to the parapet, and suddenly are looking into one of the most delightful landscapes I have ever seen: as it were, into the very virginity of hilly green country. It is all wheat-green and soft and swooping, swooping down and up, and glowing with green newness, and no houses. Down goes the declivity below us, then swerving the curve and up again, to the neighbouring hill that faces in all its greenness and long-running immaculateness. Beyond, the hills ripple away to the mountains, and far in the distance stands a round peak, that seems to have an enchanted city on its summit.

Such a pure, uprising, unsullied country, in the greenness of wheat on an April morning! - and the queer complication of hills! There seems nothing of the modern world here - no houses, no contrivances, only a sort of fair wonder and stillness, an openness which has not been violated.

The hill opposite is like a distinct companion. The near end is quite steep and wild, with evergreen oaks and scrub, and specks of black-and-white cattle on the slopes of common. But the long crest is green again with wheat, running and drooping to the south. And immediately one feels: that hill has a soul, it has a meaning.

Lying thus opposite to Tarquinia's long hill, a companion across a suave little swing of valley, one feels at once that, if this is the hill where the living Tarquinians had their gay wooden houses, then that is the hill where the dead lie buried and quick, as seeds, in their painted houses underground. The two hills are as inseparable as life and death, even now, on the sunny, green-filled April morning with the breeze blowing in from the sea. And the land beyond seems as mysterious and fresh as if it were still the morning of Time.

But Brewster wants to go back to the Palazzo Vitelleschi: it will be open now. Down the street we go, and sure enough the big doors are open, several officials are in the shadowy courtyard entrance. They salute us in the Fascist manner; *alla Romana!* Why don't they discover the Etruscan salute, and salute us *all'Etrusca!* But they are perfectly courteous and friendly. We go into the courtyard of the palace.

The museum is exceedingly interesting and delightful, to anyone who is even a bit aware of the Etruscans. It contains a great number of things found at Tarquinia, and important things.

If only we would realize it, and not tear things from their settings. Museums anyhow are wrong. But if one must have museums, let them be small, and above all, let them be local. Splendid as the Etruscan museum is in Florence, how much happier one is in the museum at Tarquinia, where all the things are Tarquinian, and at least have some association with one another, and form some sort of *organic* whole.

In an entrance room from the cortile lie a few of the long sarcophagi in which the nobles were buried. It seems as if the primitive inhabitants of this part of Italy always burned their dead, and then put the ashes in a jar, sometimes covering the jar with the dead man's helmet, sometimes with a shallow dish for a lid, and then laid the urn with its ashes in a little round grave like a little well. This is called the Villanovan[5] way of burial, in the well-tomb.

The newcomers to the country, however, apparently buried their dead whole. Here, at Tarquinia, you may still see the hills where the well-tombs of the aboriginal inhabitants are discovered, with the urns containing the ashes inside. Then come the graves where the dead were buried unburned, graves very much like those of today. But tombs of the same period with cinerary urns are found near to, or in connection. So that the new people and the old apparently lived side by side in harmony, from very early days, and the two modes of burial continued side by side, for centuries, long before the painted tombs were made.

At Tarquinia, however, the main practice seems to have been, at least from the seventh century on, that the nobles were buried in great sarcophagi, or laid out on biers, and placed in chamber-tombs, while the slaves apparently were cremated, their ashes laid in urns, and the urns often placed in the family tomb, where the stone coffins of the masters rested. The common people, on the other hand, were apparently sometimes cremated,

[5] Cf. note 1 to ch. 2.

sometimes buried in graves very much like our graves of today, though the sides were lined with stone. The mass of the common people was mixed in race, and the bulk of them were probably serf-peasants, with many half-free artisans. These must have followed their own desire in the matter of burial: some had graves, many must have been cremated, their ashes saved in an urn or jar which takes up little room in a poor man's burial-place. Probably even the less important members of the noble families were cremated, and their remains placed in the vases, which became more beautiful as the connection with Greece grew more extensive.

It is a relief to think that even the slaves - and the luxurious Etruscans had many, in historical times - had their remains decently stored in jars and laid in a sacred place. Apparently the 'vicious Etruscans' had nothing comparable to the vast dead-pits which lay outside Rome, beside the great highway, in which the bodies of slaves were promiscuously flung.

It is all a question of sensitiveness. Brute force and overbearing may make a terrific effect. But in the end, that which lives lives by delicate sensitiveness. If it were a question of brute force, not a single human baby would survive for a fortnight. It is the grass of the field, most frail of all things, that supports all life all the time. But for the green grass, no empire would rise, no man would eat bread: for grain is grass; and Hercules or Napoleon or Henry Ford would alike be denied existence.

Brute force crushes many plants. Yet the plants rise again. The Pyramids will not last a moment compared with the daisy. And before Buddha or Jesus spoke the nightingale sang, and long after the words of Jesus and Buddha are gone into oblivion the nightingale still will sing. Because it is neither preaching nor teaching nor commanding nor urging. It is just singing. And in the beginning was not a Word, but a chirrup.

Because a fool kills a nightingale with a stone, is he therefore greater than the nightingale? Because the Roman took the life out of the Etruscan, was he therefore greater than the Etruscan? Not he! Rome fell, and the Roman phenomenon with it. Italy today is far more Etruscan in its pulse than Roman; and will

always be so. The Etruscan element is like the grass of the field
and the sprouting of corn, in Italy: it will always be so. Why try
to revert to the Latin-Roman mechanism and suppression?

In the open room upon the courtyard of the Palazzo
Vitelleschi lie a few sarcophagi of stone, with the effigies carved
on top, something like the dead crusaders in English churches.
And here in Tarquinia, the effigies are more like crusaders than
usual, for some lie flat on their backs, and have a dog at their
feet; whereas usually the carved figure of the dead rears up as if
alive, from the lid of the tomb, resting upon one elbow, and
gazing out proudly, sternly. If it is a man, his body is exposed to
just below the navel, and he holds in his hand the sacred *patera*
or *mundum*, the round saucer with the raised knob in the centre,
which represents the round germ of heaven and earth[6]. It stands
for the plasm, also, of the living cell, with its nucleus, which is
the indivisible God of the beginning, and which remains alive
and unbroken to the end, the eternal quick of all things, which
yet divides and sub-divides, so that it becomes the sun of the
firmament and the lotus of the waters under the earth, and the
rose of all existence upon the earth: and the sun maintains its
own quick, unbroken for ever; and there is a living quick of the
sea, and of all the waters; and every living created thing has its
own unfailing quick. So within each man is the quick of him,
when he is a baby, and when he is old, the same quick; some
spark, some unborn and undying vivid life-electron. And this is
what is symbolized in the *patera* , which may be made to flower
like a rose or like the sun, but which remains the same, the germ
central within the living plasm.

And this *patera* , this symbol, is almost invariably found in
the hand of a dead man. But if the dead is a woman her dress

---

[6] The flat, circular shape of the so-called *patera umbilicata* of the sarcophagi, with its
characteristic knob rising in the centre, suggests to L. the possibility that this might be a
cosmic symbol, hence *mundum*. The *mundus* properly so called, however, is rather «the
well filled with the bones of sacrificial victims or pit dug with the foundations to receive
sacrificial offerings, the symbolic communication between the world of the living and
that of the dead» (Ducati 1925 I 98; Dennis 1848 and 1907 I 35 181). We may suppose
from this that L. infers a link with the *patera* of ritual libations. Applying the name
mundum to the *patera*, thought-provoking as it may be, is not sanctioned by any of the
etruscological literature current in L.'s time, much less in ours, and must therefore be
regarded as a poetic licence.

falls in soft gathers from her throat, she wears splendid jewellery, and she holds in her hand not the *mundum* , but the mirror, the box of essence, the pomegranate, some symbols of *71* her reflected nature, or of her woman's quality. But she, too, is given a proud, haughty look, as is the man: for she belongs to the sacred families that rule and that read the signs.

These sarcophagi and effigies here all belong to the centuries of the Etruscan decline, after there had been long intercourse with the Greeks, and perhaps most of them were made after the conquest of Etruria by the Romans. So that we do not look for fresh, spontaneous works of art, any more than we do in modern memorial stones. The funerary arts are always more or less commercial. The rich man orders his sarcophagus while he is still alive, and the monument-carver makes the work more or less elaborate, according to price. The figure is supposed to be a portrait of the man who orders it, so we see well enough what the later Etruscan looks like. In the third and second centuries B.C., at the fag end of their existence as a people, they look very like the Romans of the same day, whose busts we know so well. And often they are given the tiresomely haughty air of people who are no longer rulers indeed, only by the virtue of wealth.

Yet, even when the Etruscan art is Romanized and spoilt, there still flickers in it a certain naturalness and feeling. The Etruscan *Lucumones*, or prince-magistrates, were in the first place religious seers, governors in religion, then magistrates; then princes. They were not aristocrats in the Germanic sense, not even patricians in the Roman. They were first and foremost leaders in the sacred mysteries, then magistrates, then men of family and wealth. So there is always a touch of vital life, of life-significance. And you may look through modern funerary sculpture in vain for anything so good even as the *Sarcophagus of the Magistrate* , with his written scroll spread before him, his *16* strong, alert old face gazing sternly out, the necklace of office round his neck, the ring of rank on his finger. So he lies, in the museum at Tarquinia. His robe leaves him naked to the hip, and his body lies soft and slack, with the soft effect of relaxed flesh the Etruscan artists render so well, and which is so difficult. On the sculptured side of the sarcophagus the two death-dealers wield the hammer of death, the winged figures wait for the soul, and will not be persuaded away. Beautiful it is, with the easy simplicity of life. But it is late in date. Probably this old Etruscan magistrate is already an official under Roman authority: for he does not hold the sacred *mundum*, the dish, he has only the written scroll, probably of laws. As if he were no longer the religious lord or Lucumo. Though possibly, in this case, the dead man was not one of the Lucumones anyhow.

Upstairs in the museum are many vases, from the ancient crude pottery of the Villanovans to the early black ware decorated in scratches, or undecorated, called *bucchero* , and on to the painted bowls and dishes and amphoras which came from Corinth or Athens, or to those painted pots made by the Etruscans themselves more or less after the Greek patterns. These may or may not be interesting: the Etruscans are not at their best, painting dishes. Yet they must have loved them. In the early days these great jars and bowls, and smaller mixing bowls, and drinking cups and pitchers, and flat wine-cups formed a valuable part of the household treasure. In very early times the Etruscans must have sailed their ships to Corinth and to Athens, taking perhaps wheat and honey, wax and bronze-ware, iron and gold, and coming back with these precious jars, and stuffs, essences, perfumes and spice. And jars brought from overseas for the sake of their painted beauty must have been household treasures.

But then the Etruscans made pottery of their own, and by the thousand they imitated the Greek vases. So that there must have been millions of beautiful jars in Etruria. Already in the first century B.C. there was a passion among the Romans for collecting Greek and Etruscan painted jars from the Etruscans, particularly from the Etruscan tombs; jars and the little bronze votive figures and statuettes, the *sigilla Tyrrhena* of the Roman luxury. And when the tombs were first robbed, for gold and silver treasure, hundreds of fine jars must have been thrown over and smashed. Because even now, when a part-rifled tomb is discovered and opened, the fragments of smashed vases lie around.

As it is, however, the museums are full of vases. If one looks

21. Tomb of the Triclinium, discovered in 1830. 480-470 B.C. Far wall with banqueting scene, prior to removal.

22. *Tomb of the Triclinium. Right-hand wall, transferred to the Museum during the Sixties.*

23. *Reproduction of the right-hand wall of the Tomb of the Triclinium, in Weege,* Etruskische Malerei *, 1921.*

24. *Tomb of the Bacchantes, discovered in 1874. Late 6th century B.C.*
Complete end wall: cithara players and dancers.

25. *Tomb of the Dead Man, discovered in 1832. Late 6th century B.C. Detail of banqueter.*

26. *Tomb of the Lionesses, discovered in 1877. dated to around 530 B.C. Detail from the end wall: dancers, and section of the tympanum, with lioness.*

27. *Tomb of the Lionesses. Detailed from the right-hand wall: male banqueter, and frieze with duck and dolphins.*

28. *The Tomb of the Maiden, discovered in 1864. Dated to the end of the 6th century B.C. Detail from the right-hand wall, showing dancer, crater and two amphorae.*

29. *The Tomb of the Painted Vases, discovered in 1864. Dated to the late 6th century B.C. Far right-hand corner, with cavalcade.*

30. *The Tomb of the Old Man, discovered in 1864. Dated to the late 6th century B.C. Far-right hand corner, with banqueting scene.*

31. *The Tomb of the Inscriptions, discovered in 1827. Late 6th century B.C. Far left-hand corner, with cavalcade.*

32. *Tomb of the Bulls, discovered in 1892. Dated to 550-540 B.C.*
Complete end wall.

33. Tomb of the Bulls. Detail of the end wall: «un po' di pornografi-co».

34. Tomb of the Bulls. End wall, central panel: Achilles, on foot, laying an ambush for Troilus.

35. *The Arezzo Chimaera. Bronze from the late 5th to early 4th century B.C. Restored by Benvenuto Cellini. (Florence, Museo Archeologico).*

36. *The Francesca Giustiniani Tomb, discovered in 1833. Mid 5th century B.C. Complete end wall showing parting with the deceased.*

37. *Tomb of the Augurs, discovered in 1877., dated to around 530 B.C. Detail from end wall showing parting with the deceased. The person is styled* tanasar.

38. *Tomb of the Augurs. Detail from the right-hand wall: wrestlers. Left: a referee or possibly an augur.*

39. *Tomb of the Augurs. Detail from the right-hand wall the sport called* phersu: *a mastiff held on a leash fights a hooded man armed with a cudgel.*

40. *Sarcophagus of the Painted Amazon, from Tarquinia. Second half of the 4th century B.C. The side of the cover is decorated with figure Actaeon being torn apart by hounds. The chest depicts scenes of Amazon warfare. (Florence, Museo Archeologico).*

for the Greek form of elegance and convention, those elegant
'still-unravished brides of quietness'[7], one is disappointed. But
get over the strange desire we have for elegant convention, and
the vases and the dishes of the Etruscans, especially many of the
black bucchero ware, begin to open out like strange flowers,
black flowers with all the softness and the rebellion of life
against convention, or red-and-black flowers painted with
amusing free, bold designs. It is there nearly always in Etruscan
things, the naturalness verging on the commonplace, but usually
missing it, and often achieving an originality so free and bold,
and so fresh, that we, who love convention and things 'reduced
to a norm', call it a bastard art, and commonplace.

It is useless to look in Etruscan things for 'uplift'. If you
want uplift, go to the Greek and the Gothic. If you want mass,
go to the Roman. But if you love the odd spontaneous forms that
are never to be standardized, go to the Etruscans. In the
fascinating little Palazzo Vitelleschi one could spend many an
hour, but for the fact that the very fullness of museums makes
one rush through them.

---

[7] L. is referring to the opening of Keats's *Ode on a Grecian Urn*:
   Thou still unravished bride of quietness,
   Thou foster-child of Silence and slow Time,
   Sylvan historian, who canst thus express
   A flowery tale more sweetly than our rhyme...

3. THE PAINTED TOMBS OF TARQUINIA *(1)*

We arranged for the guide to take us to the painted tombs, which are the real fame of Tarquinia. After lunch we set out, climbing to the top of the town, and passing through the south-west gate, on the level hillcrest. Looking back, the wall of the town, mediaeval, with a bit of more ancient black wall lower .down, stands blank. Just outside the gate are one or two forlorn new houses, then ahead, the long, running tableland of the hill, with the white highway dipping and going on to Viterbo, inland.

«All this hill in front,» said the guide, «is tombs! All tombs! The city of the dead.»

So! Then this hill is the necropolis hill! The Etruscans never buried their dead within the city walls. And the modern cemetery and the first Etruscan tombs lie almost close up to the present city gate. Therefore, if the ancient city of Tarquinia lay on this hill, it can have occupied no more space, hardly, than the present little town of a few thousand people. Which seems impossible. Far more probably, the city itself lay on that opposite hill there, which lies splendid and unsullied, running parallel to us.

We walk across the wild bit of hilltop, where the stones crop out, and the first rock-rose flutters, and the asphodels stick up. This is the necropolis. Once it had many a tumulus, and streets *17* of tombs. Now there is no sign of any tombs: no tumulus, nothing but the rough bare hill-crest, with stones and short grass and flowers, the sea gleaming away to the right, under the sun, and the soft land inland glowing very green and pure.

But we see a little bit of wall, built perhaps to cover a water-trough. Our guide goes straight towards it. He is a fat, good-natured young man, who doesn't look as if he would be

interested in tombs. We are mistaken, however. He knows a
good deal, and has a quick, sensitive interest, absolutely
unobtrusive, and turns out to be as pleasant a companion for
such a visit as one could wish to have.

The bit of wall we see is a little hood of masonry with an
iron gate, covering a little flight of steps leading down into the
ground. One comes upon it all at once, in the rough nothingness
of the hillside. The guide kneels down to light his acetylene
lamp, and his old terrier lies down resignedly in the sun, in the
breeze which rushes persistently from the south-west, over these
long, exposed hilltops.

The lamp begins to shine and smell, then to shine without
smelling: the guide opens the iron gate, and we descend the steep
steps down the tomb. It seems a dark little hole underground: a
dark little hole, after the sun of the upper world! But the guide's
lamp begins to flare up, and we find ourselves in a little chamber
in the rock, just a small, bare little cell of a room that some
anchorite might have lived in. It is so small and bare and
familiar, quite unlike the rather splendid spacious tombs at
Cerveteri.

But the lamp flares bright, we get used to the change of light,
18 and see the paintings on the little walls. It is the *Tomb of
Hunting and Fishing*, so called from the pictures on the walls,
and it is supposed to date from the sixth century B.C. It is very
badly damaged, pieces of the wall have fallen away, damp has
eaten into the colours, nothing seems to be left. Yet in the
dimness we perceive flights of birds flying through the haze, with
the draught of life still in their wings. And as we take heart and
look closer we see the little room is frescoed all round with hazy
sky and sea, with birds flying and fishes leaping, and little men
hunting, fishing, rowing in boats. The lower part of the wall is
all a blue-green sea with a silhouette surface that ripples all
round the room. From the sea rises a tall rock, off which a naked
19 man, shadowy but still distinct, is beautifully and cleanly diving
into the sea, while a companion climbs up the rock after him,
and on the water a boat waits with rested oars in it, three men
watching the diver, the middle man standing up naked, holding
out his arms. Meanwhile a great dolphin leaps behind the boat, a

flight of birds soars upwards to pass the rock, in the clear air. Above all, from the bands of colour that border the wall at the top hang the regular loops of garlands, garlands of flowers and leaves and buds and berries, garlands which belong to maidens and to women, and which represent the flowery circle of the female life and sex. The top border of the wall is formed of horizontal stripes or ribands of colour that go all round the room, red and black and dull gold and blue and primrose, and these are the colours that occur invariably. Men are nearly always painted a darkish red, which is the colour of many Italians when they go naked in the sun, as the Etruscans went. Women are coloured paler, because women did not go naked in the sun.

At the end of the room, where there is a recess in the wall, is painted another rock rising from the sea, and on it a man with a sling is taking aim at the birds which rise scattering this way and that. A boat with a big paddle oar is holding off from the rock, a naked man amidships is giving a queer salute to the slinger, a man kneels over the bows with his back to the others, and is letting down a net. The prow of the boat has a beautifully painted eye, so the vessel shall see where it is going. In Syracuse you will see many a two-eyed boat today come swimming in to quay. One dolphin is diving down into the sea, one is leaping out. The birds fly, and the garlands hang from the border.

It is all small and gay and quick with life, spontaneous as only young life can be. If only it were not so much damaged, one would be happy, because here is the real Etruscan liveliness and naturalness. It is not impressive or grand. But if you are content with just a sense of the quick ripple of life, then here it is.

The little tomb is empty, save for its shadowy paintings. It has no bed of rock around it: only a deep niche for holding vases, perhaps vases of precious things. The sarcophagus stood on the floor, perhaps under the slinger on the end wall. And it stood álone, for this is an individual tomb, for one person only, as is usual in the older tombs of this necropolis.

In the gable triangle of the end wall, above the slinger and the boat, the space is filled in with one of the frequent Etruscan banqueting scenes of the dead. The dead man, sadly obliterated, reclines upon his banqueting couch with his flat wine-dish in his hand, resting on his elbow, and beside him, also half risen, reclines a handsome and jewelled lady in fine robes, apparently resting her left hand upon the naked breast of the man, and in her right holding up to him the garland - the garland of the female festive offering. Behind the man stands a naked slave-boy, perhaps with music, while another naked slave is just filling a wine-jug from a handsome amphora or wine-jar at the side. On the woman's side stands a maiden, apparently playing the flute: for a woman was supposed to play the flute at classic funerals; and beyond sit two maidens with garlands, one turning round to watch the banqueting pair, the other with her back to it all. Beyond the maidens in the corner are more garlands, and two birds, perhaps doves. On the wall behind the head of the banqueting lady is a problematic object, perhaps a bird-cage.

The scene is natural as life, and yet it has a heavy archaic fullness of meaning. It is the death-banquet; and at the same time it is the dead man banqueting in the underworld; for the underworld of the Etruscans was a gay place. While the living feasted out of doors, at the tomb of the dead, the dead himself feasted in like manner, with a lady to offer him garlands and slaves to bring him wine, away in the underworld. For the life on earth was so good, the life below could but be a continuance of it.

This profound belief in life, acceptance of life, seems characteristic of the Etruscans. It is still vivid in the painted tombs. There is a certain dance and glamour in all the movements, even in those of the naked slave-men. They are by no means downtrodden menials, let later Romans say what they will. The slaves in the tombs are surging with full life.

We come up the steps into the upper world, the sea-breeze and the sun. The old dog shambles to his feet, the guide blows out his lamp and locks the gate, we set off again, the dog trundling apathetic at his master's heels, the master speaking to him with that soft Italian familiarity which seems so very different from the spirit of Rome, the strong-willed Latin.

The guide steers across the hilltop, in the clear afternoon sun, towards another little hood of masonry. And one notices there is quite a number of these little gateways, built by the Government to cover the steps that lead down to the separate small tombs. It is utterly unlike Cerveteri, though the two places are not forty miles apart. Here there is no stately tumulus city, with its highroad between the tombs, and inside, rather noble, many-roomed houses of the dead. Here the little one-room tombs seem scattered at random on the hilltop, here and there: though probably, if excavations were fully carried out, here also we should find a regular city of the dead, with its streets and crossways. And probably each tomb had his little tumulus of piled earth, so that even above-ground there were streets of mounds with tomb entrances. But even so, it would be different from Cerveteri, from Caere; the mounds would be so small, the streets surely irregular. Anyhow, today there are scattered little one-room tombs, and we dive down into them just like rabbits popping down a hole. The place is a warren.

It is interesting to find it so different from Cerveteri. The Etruscans carried out perfectly what seems to be the Italian instinct: to have single, independent cities, with a certain surrounding territory, each district speaking its own dialect and feeling at home in its own little capital, yet the whole confederacy of city-states loosely linked together by a common religion and a more-or-less common interest. Even today Lucca is very different from Ferrara, and the language is hardly the same. In ancient Etruria this isolation of cities developing according to their own idiosyncrasy, within the loose union of the so-called nation, must have been complete. The contact between the plebs, the mass of the people, of Caere and Tarquinia must have been almost null. They were, no doubt, foreigners to one another. Only the Lucomones, the ruling sacred magistrates of noble family, the priests and the other nobles, and the merchants, must have kept up an intercommunion, speaking «correct» Etruscan, while the people, no doubt, spoke dialects varying so widely as to be different languages. To get any idea of the pre-Roman past we must break up the conception of oneness and uniformity, and see an endless confusion of differences.

We are diving down into another tomb, called, says the guide, the *Tomb of the Leopards*. Every tomb has been given a

name, to distinguish it from its neighbours. The tomb of the
Leopards has two spotted leopards in the triangle of the end
wall, between the roof-slopes. Hence its name.

20   The Tomb of the Leopards is a charming, cosy little room,
and the paintings on the walls have not been so very much
damaged. All the tombs are ruined to some degree by weather
and vulgar vandalism, having been left and neglected like
common holes, when they had been broken open again and
rifled to the last gasp.

But still the paintings are fresh and alive: the ochre-reds and
blacks and blues and blue-greens are curiously alive and
harmonious on the creamy yellow walls. Most of the tomb walls
have had a thin coat of stucco, but it is of the same paste as the
living rock, which is fine and yellow, and weathers to a lovely
creamy gold, a beautiful colour for a background.

The walls of this little tomb are a dance of real delight. The
room seems inhabited still by Etruscans of the sixth century
before Christ, a vivid, life-accepting people, who must have lived
with real fullness. On come the dancers and the music-players,
moving in a broad frieze towards the front wall of the tomb, the
wall facing us as we enter from the dark stairs, and where the
banquet is going on in all its glory. Above the banquet, in the
gable angle, are the two spotted leopards, heraldically facing
each other across a little tree. And the ceiling of rock has
chequered slopes of red and black and yellow and blue squares,
with a roof-beam painted with coloured circles, dark red and
blue and yellow. So that all is colour, and we do not seem to be
underground at all, but in some gay chamber of the past.

The dancers on the right wall move with a strange, powerful
alertness onwards. They are men dressed only in a loose
coloured scarf, or in the gay handsome chlamys draped as a
mantle. The *subulo*[1] plays the double flute the Etruscans loved so
much, touching the stops with big, exaggerated hands, the man
behind him touches the seven-stringed lyre, the man in front

---

[1] *subulo,-onis* a word of possible Etruscan derivation, meaning 'fife-player'- the
classical Latin expression was *tibicen,-tibicinis* (see Dennis, 1883 ed.; I, 307). In ancient
Rome, Etruscan *subulones* featured in the feast of *Quinquatrus minores*. (see Ovid *Fasti*
VI v. 651 sgg.).

turns round and signals with his left hand, holding a big wine-bowl in his right. And so they move on, on their long, sandalled feet, past the little berried olive trees, swiftly going with their limbs full of life, full of life to the tips.

This sense of vigorous, strong-bodied liveliness is characteristic of the Etruscans, and is somehow beyond art. You cannot think of art, but only life itself, as if this were the very life of the Etruscans, dancing in their coloured wraps with massive yet exuberant naked limbs, ruddy from the air and the sea-light, dancing and fluting along through the little olive trees, out in the fresh day.

The end wall has a splendid banqueting scene. The feasters recline upon a checked or tartan couch-cover, on the banqueting couch, and in the open air, for they have little trees behind them. The six feasters are bold and full of life like the dancers, but they are strong, they keep their life so beautifully and richly inside themselves, they are not loose, they don't lose themselves even in their wild moments. They lie in pairs, man and woman, reclining equally on the couch, curiously friendly. The two end women are called *hetarae*[2], courtesans; chiefly because they have yellow hair, which seems to have been a favourite feature in a woman of pleasure. The men are dark and ruddy, and naked to the waist. The women, sketched in on the creamy rock, are fair, and wear thin gowns, with rich mantles round their hips. They have a certain free bold look, and perhaps really are courtesans.

The man at the end is holding up, between thumb and forefinger, an egg, showing it to the yellow-haired woman who reclines next to him, she who is putting out her left hand as if to touch his breast. He, in his right hand, holds a large wine-dish, for the revel.

The next couple, man and fair-haired woman, are looking round and making the salute with the right hand curved over, in the usual Etruscan gesture. It seems as if they too are saluting the mysterious egg held up by the man at the end; who is, no doubt, the man who has died, and whose feast is being celebrated. But in front of the second couple a naked slave with a chaplet on his

[2] The idea is taken from Dennis (1883 ed.; I, 309). See below, note 6 ch.4.

head is brandishing an empty wine-jug, as if to say he is fetching more wine. Another slave farther down is holding out a curious thing like a little axe, or fan. The last two feasters are rather damaged. One of them is holding up a garland to the other, but not putting it over his head, as they still put a garland over your head, in India, to honour you.

Above the banqueters, in the gable angle, the two great spotted male leopards hang out their tongues and face each other heraldically, lifting a paw, on either side of a little tree. They are the leopards or panthers of the underworld Bacchus, guarding the exits and the entrances of the passion of life.

There is a mystery and a portentousness in the simple scenes which go deeper than commonplace life. It seems all so gay and light. Yet there is a certain weight, or depth of significance that goes beyond aesthetic beauty.

If one starts looking, there is much to see. But if one glances merely, there is nothing but a pathetic little room with unimposing, half-obliterated, scratchy little paintings in tempera.

There are many tombs. When we have seen one, up we go, a little bewildered, into the afternoon sun, across a tract of rough, tormented hill, and down again to the underground, like rabbits in a warren. The hilltop is really a warren of tombs. And gradually the underworld of the Etruscans becomes more real than the above day of the afternoon. One begins to live with the painted dancers and feasters and mourners, and to look eagerly for them.

21   A very lovely dance tomb is the *Tomba del Triclinio*, or *del Convito*, both of which mean: Tomb of the Feast. In size and shape this is much the same as the other tombs we have seen. It is a little chamber about fifteen feet by eleven, six feet high at the walls, about eight feet at the centre. It is again a tomb for one person, like nearly all the old painted tombs here. So there is no inner furnishing. Only the farther half of the rock-floor, the pale yellow-white rock, is raised two or three inches, and on one side of this raised part are the four holes where the feet of the sarcophagus stood. For the rest, the tomb has only its painted walls and ceiling.

And how lovely these have been, and still are! The band of

dancing figures that go round the room still is bright in colour, fresh, the women in thin spotted dresses of linen muslin and 22 coloured mantles with fine borders, the men merely in a scarf. Wildly the bacchic woman throws back her head and curves out her long, strong fingers, wild and yet contained within herself, while the broad-bodied young man turns round to her, lifting his dancing hand to hers till the thumbs all but touch. They are dancing in the open, past little trees, and birds are running, and a little fox-tailed dog is watching something with the naïve intensity of the young. Wildly and delightedly dances the next woman, every bit of her, in her soft boots and her bordered mantle, with jewels on her arms; till one remembers the old dictum, that every part of the body and of the *anima* shall know religion, and be in touch with the gods. Towards her comes the young man piping on the double flute, and dancing as he comes. He is clothed only in a fine linen scarf with a border, that hangs over his arms, and his strong legs dance of themselves, so full of life. Yet, too, there is a certain solemn intensity in his face, as he turns to the woman beyond him as she vibrates her castanets.

She is drawn fair-skinned, as all the women are, and he is of a dark red colour. That is the convention, in the tombs. But it is more than convention. In the early days men smeared themselves with scarlet when they took on their sacred natures. The Red Indians still do it. When they wish to figure in their sacred and portentous selves they smear their bodies all over with red. That must be why they are called Red Indians. In the past, for all serious or solemn occasions, they rubbed red pigment into their skins. And the same today, when they wish to put strength into their vision, and to see true, they smear round their eyes with vermilion, rubbing it into the skin. You may meet them so, in the streets of the American towns.

It is a very old custom. The American Indian will tell you: «The red paint, it is a medicine, make you see!» But he means medicine in a different sense from ours. It is deeper even than magic. Vermilion is the colour of his sacred or potent or god body. Apparently it was so in all the ancient world. Man all scarlet was his bodily godly self. We know the kings of ancient Rome, who were probably Etruscans, appeared in public with

their faces painted vermilion with minium. And Ezekiel says
(23:14-15): «She saw men pourtrayed upon the wall, the images
of the Chaldeans pourtrayed with vermilion....all of them
princes to look to, after the manner of the Babylonians of
Chaldea, the land of their nativity.»

It is then partly a convention, and partly a symbol, with the
Etruscans, to represent their men red in colour, a strong red.
Here in the tombs everything is in its sacred or inner-significant
aspect. But also the red colour is not so very unnatural. When
the Italian today goes almost naked on the beach he becomes a
lovely dark ruddy colour, dark as any Indian. And the Etruscans
went a good deal naked. The sun painted them with the sacred
minium.

The dancers dance on, the birds run, at the foot of a little
tree a rabbit crouches in a bunch, bunched with life. And on the
tree hangs a narrow, fringed scarf, like a priest's stole; another
symbol.

The end wall has a banqueting scene, rather damaged, but
still interesting. We see two separate couches, and a man and a
woman on each. The woman this time is dark-haired, so she
need not be a courtesan. The Etruscans shared the banqueting
bench with their wives, which is more than the Greeks or
Romans did, at this period. The classic world thought it indecent
for an honest woman to recline as the men did, even at the
family table. If the woman appeared at all, she must sit up
straight, in a chair.

Here, the women recline calmly with the men, and one
shows a bare foot at the end of the dark couch. In front of the
lecti , the couches, is in each case a little low square table bearing
delicate dishes of food for the feasters. But they are not eating.
One woman is lifting her hand to her head in a strange salute to
the robed piper at the end, the other woman seems with the
lifted hand to be saying No! to the charming maid, perhaps a
servant, who stands at her side, presumably offering the
alabastron, or ointment-jar, while the man at the end is
apparently holding up an egg. Wreaths hang from the ivy-border
above, a boy is bringing a wine-jug, the music goes on, and
under the beds a cat is on the prowl, while an alert cock watches

him. The silly partridge, however, turns his back, stepping innocently along.

This lovely tomb has a pattern of ivy and ivy berries, the ivy of the underworld Bacchus, along the roof-beam and in a border round the top of the walls. The roof-slopes are chequered in red and black, white, blue, brown and yellow squares. In the gable angle, instead of the heraldic beasts, two naked men are sitting reaching back to the centre of an ivy-covered altar, arm outstretched across the ivy. But one man is almost obliterated. At the foot of the other man, in the tight angle of the roof, is a pigeon, the bird of the soul that coos out of the unseen.

This tomb has been open since 1830, and is still fresh. It is interesting to see, in Fritz Weege's book, *Etruskische Malerei*, a   23
reproduction of an old water-colour drawing of the dancers on the right wall. It is a good drawing, yet, as one looks closer, it is quite often out, both in line and position. These Etruscan paintings, not being in our convention, are very difficult to copy. The picture shows my rabbit all spotted, as if it were some queer cat. And it shows a squirrel in the little tree in front of the piper, and flowers, and many details that have now disappeared.

But it is a good drawing, unlike some that Weege reproduces, which are so Flaxmanised and Greekified; and made according to what our great-grandfathers thought they *ought* to be, as to be really funny, and a warning for ever against thinking how things *ought* to be, when already they are quite perfectly what they are.

We climb up to the world, and pass for a few minutes through the open day. Then down we go again. In the *Tomb of the Bacchanti* the colours have almost gone. But still we see, on   24
the end wall, a strange wondering dancer out of the mists of time carrying his zither, and beyond him, beyond the little tree, a man of the dim ancient world, a man with a short beard, strong and mysteriously male, is reaching for a wild archaic maiden who throws up her hands and turns back to him her excited, subtle face. It is wonderful, the strength and mystery of old life that comes out of these faded figures. The Etruscans are still there, upon the wall.

Above the figures, in the gable angle, two spotted deer are

prancing heraldically towards one another, on either side the altar, and behind them two dark lions, with pale manes and with tongues hanging out, are putting up a paw to seize them on the haunch. So the old story repeats itself.

From the striped border rude garlands are hanging, and on the roof are little painted stars, or four-petalled flowers. So much has vanished! Yet even in the last breath of colour and form, how much life there is!

In the *Tomba del Morto,* the Tomb of the Dead Man, the banqueting scene is replaced by a scene, apparently, of a dead man on his bed, with a woman leaning gently over to cover his face. It is almost like a banquet scene. But it is so badly damaged! In the gable above, two dark heraldic lions are lifting the paw against two leaping, frightened, backward-looking birds. This is a new variation. On the broken wall are the dancing legs of a man, and there is more life in these Etruscan legs, fragment as they are, than in the whole bodies of men today. Then there is one really impressive dark figure of a naked man who throws up his arms so that his great wine-bowl stands vertical, and with spread hand and closed face gives a strange gesture of finality. He has a chaplet on his head, and a small pointed beard, and lives there shadowy and significant.

Lovely again is the *Tomba delle Leonesse*, the Tomb of the Lionesses. In its gable two spotted lionesses swing their bell-like udders, heraldically facing one another across the altar. Beneath is a great vase, and a flute-player playing to it on one side, a zither-player on the other, making music to its sacred contents. Then on either side of these goes a narrow frieze of dancers, very strong and lively in their prancing. Under the frieze of dancers is a lotus dado, and below that again, all round the room, the dolphins are leaping, leaping all downwards into the rippling sea, while birds fly between the fishes.

On the right wall reclines a very impressive dark red man wearing a curious cap, or head-dress, that has long tails like long plaits. In his right hand he holds up an egg, and in his left is the shallow wine-bowl of the feast. The scarf or stole of his human office hangs from a tree before him, and the garland of his human delight hangs at his side. He holds up the egg of resurrection, within which the germ sleeps as the soul sleeps in the tomb, before it breaks the shell and emerges again. There is another reclining man, much obliterated, and beside him hangs a garland or chain like the chains of dandelion-stems we used to make as children. And this man has a naked flute-boy, lovely in naked outline, coming towards him.

The *Tomba della Pulcella*, or Tomb of the Maiden, has 28 faded but vigorous figures at the banquet, and very ornate couch-covers in squares and the key-pattern, and very handsome mantles.

The *Tomba dei Vasi Dipinti*, Tomb of the Painted Vases, 29 has great amphorae painted on the side wall, and springing towards them is a weird dancer, the ends of his waist-cloth flying. The amphorae, two of them, have scenes painted on them, which can still be made out. On the end wall is a gentle little banquet scene, the bearded man softly touching the woman with him under the chin, a slave-boy standing childishly behind, and an alert dog under the couch. The *kylix* , or wine-bowl, that the man holds is surely the biggest on record; exaggerated, no doubt, to show the very special importance of the feast. Rather gentle and lovely is the way he touches the woman under the chin, with a delicate caress. That again is one of the charms of the Etruscan paintings: they really have the sense of touch; the people and the creatures are all really in touch. It is one of the rarest qualities, in life as well as in art. There is plenty of pawing and laying hold, but no real touch. In pictures especially, the people may be in contact, embracing or laying hands on one another. But there is no soft flow of touch. The touch does not come from the middle of the human being. It is merely a contact of surfaces, and juxtaposition of objects. This is what makes so many of the great masters boring, in spite of all their clever composition. Here, in this faded Etruscan painting, there is a quiet flow of touch that unites the man and the woman on the couch, the timid boy behind, the dog that lifts his nose, even the very garlands that hang from the wall.

Above the banquet, in the triangle, instead of lions or leopards, we have the hippocampus, a favourite animal of the Etruscan imagination. It is a horse that ends in a long, flowing fish tail. Here these two hippocampi face one another prancing their front legs, while their fish-tails flow away into the narrow angle of the roof. They are a favourite symbol of the seaboard Etruscans.

30   In the *Tomba del Vecchio*, the Tomb of the Old Man, a beautiful woman with her hair dressed backwards into the long cone of the East, so that her head is like a sloping acorn, offers her elegant, twisted garland to the white-bearded old man, who is now beyond garlands. He lifts his left hand up at her, with the rich gesture of these people, that must mean something each time.

Above them, the prancing spotted deer are being seized in the haunch by two lions. And the waves of obliteration, wastage of time and damage of men, are silently passing over all.

So we go on, seeing tomb after tomb, dimness after dimness, divided between the pleasure of finding so much and the disappointment that so little remains. One tomb after another, and nearly everything faded or eaten away, or corroded with alkali, or broken wilfully. Fragments of people at banquets, limbs that dance without dancers, birds that fly in nowhere, lions whose devouring heads are devoured away! Once it was all bright and dancing: the delight of the underworld; honouring the dead with wine, and flutes playing for a dance, and limbs whirling and pressing. And it was deep and sincere honour rendered to the dead and to the mysteries. It is contrary to our ideas; but the ancients had their own philosophy for it. As the pagan old writer says: «For no part of us nor of our bodies shall be, which doth not feel religion: and let there be no lack of singing for the soul, no lack of leaping and of dancing for the knees and heart; for all these know the gods.»

Which is very evident in the Etruscan dancers. They know the gods in their very finger-tips. The wonderful fragments of limbs and bodies that dance on in a field of obliteration still know the gods, and make it evident to us.

But we can hardly see any more tombs. The upper air seems pallid and bodiless, as we emerge once more, white with the light of the sea and the coming evening. And spent and slow the old dog rises once more to follow after.

We decide that the *Tomba delle Iscrizioni*, the Tomb of the Inscriptions, shall be our last for today. It is dim but fascinating, 31 as the lamp flares up, and we see in front of us the end wall, painted with a false door studded with pale studs, as if it led to another chamber beyond; and riding from the left, a trail of shadowy tall horsemen; and running in from the right, a train of wild shadowy dancers wild as demons.

The horsemen are naked on the four naked horses, and they make gestures as they come towards the painted door. The horses are alternately red and black, the red having blue manes and hoofs, the black, red ones, or white. They are tall archaic horses on slim legs, with necks arched like a curved knife. And they come pinking daintily and superbly along, with their long tails, towards the dark red death-door.

From the left, the stream of dancers leaps wildly, playing music, carrying garlands or wine-jugs, lifting their arms like revellers, lifting their live knees, and signalling with their long hands. Some have little inscriptions written near them: their names.

And above the false door in the angle of the gable is a fine design: two black, wide-mouthed, pale-maned lions seated back to back, their tails rising like curved stems, between them, as they each one lift a black paw against the cringing head of a cowering spotted deer, that winces to the death-blow. Behind each deer is a smaller dark lion, in the acute angle of the roof, coming up to bite the shrinking deer in the haunch, and so give the second death-wound. For the wounds of death are in the neck and in the flank.

At the other end of the tomb are wrestlers and gamesters but so shadowy now ! We cannot see any more, nor look any farther in the shadows for the unconquerable life of the Etruscans, whom the Romans called vicious, but whose life, in these tombs, is certainly fresh and clearly vivid.

The upper air is wide and pale, and somehow void. We cannot see either world any more, the Etruscan underworld nor the common day. Silently, tired, we walk back in the wind to the town, the old dog padding stoically behind. And the guide promises to take us to the other tombs to-morrow.

There is a haunting quality in the Etruscan representations. Those leopards with their long tongues hanging out: those flowing hippocampi; those cringing spotted deer, struck in flank and neck; they get into the imagination, and will not go out. And as we see the wavy edge of the sea, the dolphins curving over, the diver going down clean, the little man climbing up the rock after him so eagerly. Then the men with beards who recline on the banqueting beds: how they hold up the mysterious egg! And the women with the conical head-dress, how strangely they lean forward, with caresses we no longer know! The naked slaves joyfully stoop to the wine-jars. Their nakedness is its own clothing, more easy than drapery. The curves of their limbs show pure pleasure in life, pleasure that goes deeper still in the limbs of the dancers, in the big, long hands thrown out and dancing to the very ends of the fingers, a dance which surges from within, like a current in the sea. It is as if the current of some strong different life swept through them, different from our shallow current today: as if they drew their vitality from different depths that we are denied.

Yet in a few centuries they lost their vitality. The Romans took the life out of them. It seems as if the power of resistance to life, self-assertive and overbearing, such as the Romans knew: a power which must needs be moral, or carry morality with it, as a cloak for its inner ugliness: would always succeed in destroying the natural flowering of life. And yet there still are a few wild flowers and creatures.

The natural flowering of life! It is not so easy for human beings as it sounds. Behind all the Etruscan liveliness was a religion of life, which the chief men were seriously responsible for. Behind all the dancing was a vision, and even a science of life, a conception of the universe and man's place in the universe which made men live to the depth of their capacity.

To the Etruscan all was alive; the whole universe lived; and the business of man was to live amid it all. He had to draw life into himself, out of the wandering huge vitalities of the world. The cosmos was alive, like a vast creature. The whole thing breathed and stirred. Evaporation went up like breath from the nostrils of a whale, steaming up. The sky received it in its blue bosom, breathed it in and pondered on it and transmuted it, before breathing it out again. Inside the earth were fires like the heat in the hot red liver of a beast. Out of the fissures of the earth came breaths of other breathing, vapours direct from the living physical underearth, exhalations carrying inspiration. The whole thing was alive, and had a great soul or *anima*: and in spite of one great soul, there were myriad roving, lesser souls: every man, every creature and tree and lake and mountain and stream, was animate, had its own peculiar consciousness. And it has today.

The cosmos was one, and its *anima* was one; but it was made up of creatures. And the greatest creature was earth, with its soul of inner fire. The sun was only a reflection, or off-throw, or brilliant handful, of the great inner fire. But in juxtaposition to earth lay the sea, the waters that moved and pondered and held a deep of their own. Earth and waters lay side by side, together and utterly different.

So it was. The universe, which was a single aliveness with a single soul, instantly changed, the moment you thought of it, and became a dual creature with two souls, fiery and watery, for ever mingling and rushing apart, and held by the great aliveness of the universe in an ultimate equilibrium. But they rushed together and they rushed apart, and immediately they became myriad: volcanoes and seas, then streams and mountains, trees, creatures, men. And everything was dual, or contained its own duality, for ever mingling and rushing apart.

The old idea of the vitality of the universe was evolved long before history begins, and elaborated into a vast religion before we get a glimpse of it. When history does begin, in China or India, Egypt, Babylonia, even in the Pacific and aboriginal America, we see evidence of one underlying religious idea: the conception of the vitality of the cosmos, the myriad vitalities in vast confusion, which still is held in some sort of array: and man amid all the glowing welter, adventuring, struggling, striving for one thing, life, vitality, more vitality: to get into himself more of the gleaming vitality of the cosmos. That is the treasure. The active religious idea was that man, by vivid attention and subtlety and exerting all his strength, could draw more life into himself, more life, more and more glistening vitality, till he became shining like the morning, blazing like a god. When he was all himself he painted himself vermillion like the throat of dawn, and was god's body, visibly, red and utterly vivid. So he was a prince, a king, a god, an Etruscan Lucumo; Pharaoh, or Belshazzar, or Ashurbanipal, or Tarquin; in a feebler *decrescendo*, Alexander, or Caesar or Napoleon.

This was the idea at the back of all the great old civilizations. It was even, half-transmuted, at the back of David's mind and voiced in the Psalms. But with David the living cosmos became merely a personal god. With the Egyptians and Babylonians and Etruscans, strictly there were no personal gods. There were only idols or symbols. It was the living cosmos itself, dazzlingly and gaspingly complex, which was divine, and which could be contemplated only by the strongest soul, and only at moments. And only the peerless soul could draw into itself some last flame from the quick. Then you had a king-god indeed.

There you have the ancient idea of kings, who are gods by vividness, because they have gathered into themselves core after core of vital potency from the universe, till they are clothed in scarlet, they are bodily a piece of the deepest fire. Pharaohs and kings of Niniveh, kings of the East, and Etruscan Lucumones, they are the living clue to the pure fire, to the cosmic vitality. They are the vivid key of life, the vermillion clue to the mystery and the delight of death and life. They, in their own body, unlock the vast treasure house of the cosmos for their people, and bring out life, and show the way into the dark of death, which is the blue burning of the one fire. They, in their own bodies, are the life-bringers and the death-guides, leading ahead in the dark, and coming out in the day with more than sunlight in their bodies. Can one wonder that such dead are wrapped in gold; or were?

The life-bringers, and the death-guides. But they set guards at the gates both of life and death. They keep the secrets, and safeguard the way. Only a few are initiated into the mystery of the bath of life, and the bath of death, the pool within pool within pool, wherein, when a man is dipped, he becomes darker than blood, with death, and brighter than fire, with life; till at last he is scarlet royal as a piece of living life, pure vermillion.

The people are not initiated into the cosmic ideas, nor into the awakened throb of more vivid consciousness. Try as you may, you can never make the mass of men throb with full awakenedness. They *cannot* be more than a little aware. So you must give them symbols, ritual and gesture, which will fill their body with life up to their own full measure. Any more is fatal. And so the actual knowledge must be guarded from them, lest knowing the formulae, without undergoing at all the experience that corresponds, they may become insolent and impious, thinking they have the all, when they have only an empty monkey-chatter. The esoteric knowledge will always be esoteric, since knowledge is an experience, not a formula. But it is foolish to hand out the formulae. A little knowledge is indeed a dangerous thing. No age proves it more than ours. Monkey-chatter is at last the most disastrous of things.

The clue to the Etruscan life was the Lucumo, the religious prince. Beyond him were the priests and warriors. Then came the people and the slaves. People and warriors and slaves did not think about religion. There would soon have been no religion left. They felt the symbols and danced the sacred dances. For they were always kept *in touch*, physically, with the mysteries. The 'touch' went from the Lucumo down to the merest slave. The blood-stream was unbroken. But 'knowing' belonged to the high-born, the pure-bred.

So, in the tombs we find only the simple, uninitiated vision of the people. There is none of the priest-work of Egypt. The symbols are to the artist just wonder-forms, pregnant with emotion and good for decoration. It is so all the way through Etruscan art. The artists evidently were of the people, artisans. Presumably they were of the old Italic stock, and understood nothing of the religion in its intricate form, as it had come in from the East: though doubtless the crude principles of the official religion were the same as those of the primitive religion of the aborigines. The same crude principles ran through the religion of all the barbaric world of that time, Druid or Teutonic or Celtic. But the newcomers in Etruria held secret the science and philosophy of their religion, and gave the people the symbols and the ritual, leaving the artists free to use the symbols as they would; which shows that there was no priest-rule.

Later, when scepticism came over all the civilized world, as it did after Socrates, the Etruscan religion began to die, Greeks and Greek rationalism flooded in, and Greek stories more or less took the place of the old Etruscan symbolic thought. Then again the Etruscan artists, uneducated, used the Greek stories as they had used the Etruscan symbols, quite freely, making them over again just to please themselves.

But one radical thing the Etruscan people never forgot, because it was in their blood as well as in the blood of their masters: and that was the mystery of the journey out of life, and into death; the death journey, and the sojourn in the after-life. The wonder of their soul continued to play round the mystery of this journey and of this sojourn.

In the tombs we see it, throes of wonder and vivid feeling throbbing over death. Man moves naked and glowing through the universe. Then comes death: he dives into the sea, he departs into the underworld.

The sea is that vast primordial creature that has a soul also, whose inwardness is womb of all things, out of which all things emerged, and into which they are devoured back. Balancing the sea is the earth of inner fire, of after-life and before-life. Beyond the waters and the ultimate fire lay only that oneness of which the people knew nothing: it was a secret the Lucumones kept for themselves, as they kept the symbol of it in their hand.

But the sea the people knew. The dolphin leaps in and out of it suddenly, as a creature that suddenly exists, out of nowhere. He was not: and lo! there he is! The dolphin which gives up the sea's rainbows only when he dies. Out he leaps; then, with a head-dive, back again he plunges into the sea. He is so much alive, he is like the phallus carrying the fiery spark of procreation down into the wet darkness of the womb. The diver does the same, carrying like a phallus his small hot spark into the deeps of death. And the sea will give up her dead like dolphins that leap out and have the rainbow within them.

But the duck that swims on the water, and lift his wings, is another matter: the blue duck, or goose, so often represented by the Etruscans. He is the same goose that saved Rome, in the night.

The duck does not live down within the waters as the fish does. The fish is the *anima*, the animate life, the very clue to the vast sea, the watery element to the first submission. For this reason Jesus was represented in the first Christian centuries as a fish, in Italy especially, where the people still thought in the Etruscan symbols. Jesus was the *anima* of the vast, moist ever-yielding element which was the opposite and the counterpart of the red flame the Pharaohs and the kings of the East had sought to invest themselves with.

But the duck had no such subaqueous nature as the fish. It swims upon the waters, and is hot-blooded, belonging to the red-flame of the animal body of life. But it dives under water, and preens itself upon the flood. So it became, to man, the symbol of that part of himself which delights in the waters, and dives in, and rises up and shakes its wings. It is a symbol of a man's own phallus and phallic life. So you see a man holding on his hand the hot, soft, alert duck, offering it to the maiden. So today, the Red-Indian makes a secret gift to the maiden of a hollow, earthenware duck, in which is a little fire and incense. It is that part of his body and his fiery little life that a man can offer to a maid. And it is that awareness or alertness in him, that other consciousness, that wakes in the night and rouses the city.

But the maid offers the man a garland, the rim of flowers from the edge of the 'pool', which can be placed over the man's head and laid on his shoulders, in symbol that he is invested with the power of the maiden's mystery and different strength, the female power. For whatever is laid on the shoulders is a sign of power added.

Birds fly on the walls of the tombs. The artist must often have seen these priests, the augurs, with their crooked, bird-headed staffs in their hand, out on a high place watching the flight of larks or pigeons across the quarters of the sky. They were reading the signs and portents, looking for an indication, how they should direct the course of some serious affair. To us it may seem foolish. To them, hot-blooded birds flew through the

breast of a man, or as thoughts fly through the mind. In their
flight the suddenly roused birds, or the steady, far-coming birds,
moved wrapped in a deeper consciousness, in the complex
destiny of all things. And since all things corresponded in the
ancient world, and man's bosom mirrored itself in the bosom of
the sky, or *vice versa*, the birds were flying to a portentous goal,
in the man's breast who watched, as well as flying their own way
in the bosom of the sky. If the augur could see the birds flying *in
his heart*, then he would know which way destiny too was flying
for him.

The science of augury certainly was no exact science. But it
was as exact as our sciences of psychology or political economy.
And the augurs were as clever as our politicians, who also must
practice divination, if ever they are to do anything worth the
name. There is no other way when you are dealing with life. And
if you live by the cosmos, you look in the cosmos for your clue.
If you live by a personal god, you pray to him. If you are
rational, you think things over. But it all amounts to the same
thing in the end. Prayer, or thought, or studying the stars, or
watching the flight of birds, or studying the entrails of sacrifice,
it is all the same process, ultimately: of divination. All it depends
on is the amount of *true*, sincere, religious concentration you can
bring to bear on your object. An act of pure attention, if you are
capable of it, will bring its own answer. And you choose that
object to concentrate upon which will best focus your consciousness. Every real discovery made, every serious and significant
decision ever reached, was reached and made by divination. The
souls stirs, and makes an act of pure attention, and that is a
discovery.

The science of the augur and the haruspex was not so foolish
as our modern science of political economy. If the hot liver of the
victim cleared the soul of the haruspex, and made him capable of
that ultimate inward attention which alone tells us the last thing
we need to know, then why quarrel with the haruspex? To him,
the universe was alive, and in quivering *rapport*. To him, the
blood was conscious: he thought with his heart. To him, the
blood was the red and shining stream of consciousness itself.
Hence, to him, the liver, that great organ where the blood

struggles and 'overcomes death', was an object of profound mystery and significance. It stirred his soul and purified his consciousness; for it was also his victim. So he gazed into the hot liver, that was mapped out in the fields and regions like the sky of stars, but these fields and regions were those of the red, shining consciousness that runs through the whole animal creation. And therefore it must contain the answer to his own blood's question.

It is the same with the study of stars, or the sky of stars. Whatever object will bring the consciousness into a state of pure attention, in a time of perplexity, will also give back an answer to the perplexity. But it is truly a question of *divination*. As soon as there is any pretence of infallibility, and pure scientific calculation, the whole thing becomes a fraud and a jugglery. But the same is true not only of augury and astrology, but also of prayer and pure reason, and even of the discoveries of the great laws and principles of science. Men juggle with prayer today as once they juggled with augury; and in the same way they are juggling with science. Every great discovery or decision comes by an act of divination. Facts are fitted round afterwards. But all attempts at divination, even prayer and reason and research itself, lapse into jugglery when the heart looses its purity. In the impurity of his heart, Socrates often juggled logic unpleasantly. And no doubt, when scepticism came over the ancient world, the haruspex and the augur became jugglers and pretenders. But for centuries they held real sway. It is amazing to see, in Livy[3], what a big share they must have had in the building up of the great Rome of the Republic.

Turning from birds to animals, we find in the tombs the continual repetition of lion against deer. As soon as the world was created, according to the ancient idea, it took on duality. All

---

[3] Livy (V, 15-17) tells that the Romans, engaged in the siege of Veii (396 B.C.) abducted an old Etruscan haruspex to explain the ominous waxing of the waters in the lake of Albano. It was in fact the Roman custom to make use of Etruscan seers, which were then in short supply because of the war. Later (V, 51-52), when in Rome it is debated upon the opportunity of moving the site of the city to that of Veii, Camillus manages to persuade the people to stay on by recalling the sacredness of the choice of the site, and of the foundation *etrusco ritu*, in accordance to fatal omens.

things became dual, not only in the duality of sex, but in the polarity of action. This is the 'impious pagan duality'. It did not, however, contain the later pious duality of good and evil.

The leopard and the deer, the lion and the bull, the cat and the dove, or the partridge, these are part of the great duality, or polarity of the animal kingdom. But they do not represent good action and evil action. On the contrary, they represent the polarised activity of the divine cosmos, in its animal creation.

The treasure of treasures is the soul, which, in every creature, in every tree or pool, means that mysterious conscious point of balance or equilibrium between the two halves of the duality, the fiery and the watery. This mysterious point clothes itself in vividness after vividness from the right hand, and vividness after vividness from the left. And in death it does not disappear, but is stored in the egg, or in the jar, or even in the tree which brings it forth again.

But the soul itself, the conscious spark of every creature, is not dual; and being immortal, it is also the altar on which our immortality and our duality is at last sacrificed.

So as the key picture in the tombs, we have over and over again the heraldic beasts facing one another across the altar, or the tree, or the vase; and the lion is smiting the deer in hip and throat. The deer is spotted, for day and night, the lion is dark and light the same.

The deer or lamb or goat or cow is the gentle creature with udder of overflowing milk and fertility; or it is the stag or ram or bull, the great father of the herd, with horns of power set obvious on the brow, and indicating the dangerous aspect of the beast of fertility. These are the creatures of prolific, boundless procreation, the beasts of peace and increase. So even Jesus is the lamb. And the endless, endless gendering of these creatures will fill the earth with cattle till herds rub flanks all over the world, and hardly a tree can rise between.

But this must not be so, since they are only half, even of the animal creation. Balance must be kept. And this is the altar we are all sacrificed upon: it is even death; just as it is our soul and purest treasure.

So, on the other hand from the deer, we have lionesses and

leopards. These, too, are male and female. These, too, have udders of milk and nourish young; as the wolf nourished the first Romans: prophetically, as the destroyers of many deer, including the Etruscan. So these fierce ones guard the treasure and the gateway, which the prolific ones would squander or close up with too much gendering. They bite the deer in neck and haunch, where the great blood-streams run.

So the symbolism goes all through the Etruscan tombs. It is very much the symbolism of all the ancient world. But here it is not exact and scientific, as in Egypt. It is simple and rudimentary, and the artist plays with it as a child with fairy stories. Nevertheless, it is the symbolic element which rouses the deeper emotion, and gives the peculiarly satisfying quality to the dancing figures and the creatures. A painter like Sargent, for example, is so clever. But in the end he is utterly uninteresting, a bore. He never has an inkling of his own triviality and silliness. One Etruscan leopard, even one little quail, is worth all the miles of him.

4. THE PAINTED TOMBS OF TARQUINIA (2)

We sit at the tin tables of the café above the gate watching the peasants coming in the evening from the fields, with their implements and their asses. As they drift in through the gate the 'man of the *Dazio*, the town customs, watches them, asks them questions if they carry bundles, prods the pack on the ass, and when a load of brushwood rolls up keeps it halted while he pierces the load with a long steel rod, carefully thrusting to see if he can feel hidden barrels of wine or demijohns of oil, bales of oranges or any other food-stuffs. Because all food-stuffs that come into an Italian town - many other things too, besides comestibles - must pay a duty, in some instances a heavy one.

Probably in Etruscan days the peasants came in very much the same, at evening, to the town. The Etruscans were instinctively citizens. Even the peasants dwelt within walls. And in those days, no doubt, the peasants were serfs very much as they are today in Italy, working the land for no wages, but for a portion of the produce and working the land intensely, with that careful, almost passionate attention the Italian still gives to the soil; and living in the city, or village, but having straw huts out in the fields, for summer.

But in those days, on a fine evening like this, the men would come in naked, darkly ruddy-coloured from the sun and wind, with strong, insouciant bodies; and the women would drift in, wearing the loose, becoming smock of white or blue linen and somebody, surely, would be playing on the pipes; and somebody, surely, would be singing, because the Etruscans had a passion for music, and an inner carelessness the modern Italians have lost. The peasants would enter the clear, clean, sacred space inside the gates, and salute the gay-coloured little temple as they passed along the street that rose uphill towards the arx, between rows of low houses with gay-coloured fronts painted or hung with bright terra-cottas. One can almost hear them still, calling, shouting, piping, singing, driving in the mixed flocks of sheep and goats, that go silently, and leading the slow, white, ghostlike oxen with the yokes still on their necks.

And surely, in those days, young nobles would come splashing in on horseback, riding with naked limbs on an almost naked horse, carrying probably a spear, and cantering ostentatiously through the throng of red-brown, full-limbed, smooth-skinned peasants. A Lucumo, even, sitting very noble in his chariot driven by an erect charioteer, might be driving in at sundown, halting before the temple to perform the brief ritual of entry into the city. And the crowding populace would wait; for the Lucumo of the old days, glowing ruddy in flesh, his beard stiffly trimmed in the Oriental style, the torque of gold round his neck, and the mantle or wrap bordered with scarlet falling in full folds, leaving the breast bare, he was divine, sitting on the chair in his chariot in the stillness of power. The people drew strength even from looking at him.

The chariot drew a little forward, from the temple; the Lucumo, sitting erect on his chair in the chariot, and bare-shouldered and bare-breasted, waits for the people. Then the peasants would shrink back in fear. But perhaps some citizen in a white tunic would lift up his arm in salute, and come forward to state his difficulty, or to plead for justice. And the Lucumo, seated silent within another world of power, disciplined to his own responsibility of knowledge for the people, would listen to the end. Then a few words - and the chariot of gilt bronze swirls off up the hill to the house of the chief, the citizens drift on their houses, the music sounds in the dark streets, torches flicker, the whole place is eating, feasting, and as far as possible having a gay time.

It is different now. The drab peasants, muffled in ugly clothing, straggle in across the waste bit of space, and trail home, songless and meaningless. We have lost the art of living;

and in the most important science of all, the science of daily life, the science of behaviour, we are complete ignoramuses. We have psychology instead. Today in Italy, in the hot Italian summer, if a navvy working in the streets takes off his shirt to work with free naked torso, a policeman rushes to him and commands him insultingly into his shirt again. One would think a human being was such a foul indecency altogether that life was feasible only when the indecent thing was as far as possible blotted out. The very exposure of female arms and legs in the street is only done as an insult to the whole human body. «Look at that! It doesn't matter!»

Neither does it! But then, why did the torso of the workman matter?

At the hotel, in the dark emptiness of the place, there are three Japanese staying: little yellow men. They have come to inspect the salt works down on the coast below Tarquinia, so we are told, and they have a Government permit. The salt works, the extracting of salt from the pools shut off from the low sea, are sort of prisons, worked by convict labour. One wonders why Japanese men should want to inspect such places, officially. But we are told that these salt works are 'very important'.

Albertino is having a very good time with the three Japanese, and seems to be very deep in their confidence, bending over their table, his young brown head among the three black ones, absorbed and on the *chi vive*. He rushes off for their food - then rushes to us to see what we want to eat.

«What is there?»

«Er - c'è-» He always begins with wonderful deliberation as if there was a menu fit for the Tsar. Then he breaks off suddenly, says: «I'll ask the mamma!» - darts away - returns, and says exactly what we knew he'd say, in a bright voice, as if announcing the New Jerusalem: «There are eggs - er - and beefsteak-*er* and there are some little potatoes». We know the eggs and beefsteak well! However, I decide to have beefsteak once more, with the little potatoes - left over by good fortune from lunch-fried. Off darts Albertino, only to dart back and announce that the potatoes and beefsteak are finished («by the Chinese,» he whispers), but there are the frogs. «There are what?» «*Le rane,* the frogs!» «What sort of frogs?» «I'll show you!» Off he darts again, returns with a plate containing eight or nine pairs of frogs' naked hind-legs. Brewster looks the other way and I accept frogs - they look quite good. In the joy of getting the frogs safely to port, Albertino skips, and darts off: to return in a moment with a bottle of beer, and whisper to us all the information about the Chinese, as he calls them. They can't speak a word of Italian. When they want a word they take the little book, French and Italian. *Bread?* - eh? They want bread. Er! - Albertino gives little grunts, like commas and semicolons, which I write as *er!* Bread they want, eh? - er! - they take the little book - here he takes an imaginary little book, lays it on the tablecloth, wets his finger and turns over the imaginary leaves - *bread!* er!- 'p' - you look under 'p' - er!-*ecco! pane!-pane! - si capisce!* - bread! they want bread. Then wine! er! take the little book (he turns over imaginary little leaves with fervour) - er! here you are, *vino!-pane, e vino!* So they do! Every word! They looked out name! Er! you! Er! I tell him, *Albertino.* And so the boy continues, till I ask what about *le rane?* Ah! *Er! Le rane!* Off he darts, and swirls back with a plate of fried frog's legs, in pairs.

He is an amusing and vivacious boy, yet underneath a bit sad and wistful, with all his responsibility. The following day he darted to show us a book of views of Venice, left behind by the Chinese, as he persists in calling them, and asks if I want it. I don't. Then he shows us two Japanese postage stamps, and the address of one of the Japanese gentlemen, written on a bit of paper. The Japanese gentleman and Albertino are to exchange picture postcards. I insist that the Japanese are not Chinese. «Er!» says Albertino. «But the Japanese are also Chinese!» I insist that they are not, that they live in a different country. He darts off, and returns with a school atlas. He is really an intelligent boy, and ought to be going to school instead of running an hotel at the tender age of fourteen.

The guide to the tombs, having had to keep watch at the museum all night, wants to get a sleep after dawn, so we are not to start till ten. The town is already empty, the people gone out to the fields. A few men stand about with nothing doing. The

41. *Tomb of the Baron, discovered in 1827, dated to around 500 B.C. End wall: parting with deceased.*

42. *Tomb of the Typhon, discovered in 1832. Painting on the central pilaster: snake-footed figure or «typhon». First half of the second century B.C.*

43. *Tomb of the Shields, discovered in 1870, dated to around the mid 4th century B.C. Central chamber with banqueting scene at left.*

44. Tomb of the Shields. Couple banqueting: the woman is handing the man an egg. Detail from the left-hand wall.

45. *First Tomb of Orcus, discovered in 1868. Early 4th century B.C. Head of a girl of the Velchas family. Detail, now in the Museo Nazionale, Tarquinia.*

46. *Porta Nuova and cliffs, on the east side of the medieval town, which looks across towards the Etruscan necropolis.*

47. *Tarquinia in the 'Twenties. Porta Castello. Entrance into the town from the north, between the first and the second circuit of walls.*

48. *Tarquinian carters.*

49. *The towers of Tarquinia, looking south.*

*Montalto di Castro - Capanna di Pecorai
(dove si produce la rinomata ricotta romana)*

50. *The Maremma near Montalto di Castro. Dairy on a large ranch in
the Twenties.*

51. Early farm machine, around 1900.

52. *Open ranching of cattle, with watering-place and mounted herdsman.*

Montalto di Castro
Caccie nelle Tenute del Marchese Giacinto Guglielmi

53. *Boar-hunting in the Maremma.*

54. *The bridge over the Fiora, known as the «Abbadia» or «devil's» bridge, with the 12th century frontier fortress, close to the site of ancient Vulci.*

55. *Preparing a wood-pile for charcoal-making: a team of charcoal burners in the Vulci area during the 'Twenties.*

56. *The wood-pile completed.*

57. *The finished product: sacks of charcoal.*

58. Asphodelus ramosus, *the asphodel. One of the Liliaceae, regarded by the ancient as the flower of the dead.*

city gates are wide open. At night they are closed, so that the
Dazio man can sleep: and you can neither get in nor out of the
town. We drink still another coffee - Albertino's morning dose
was a very poor show.

Then we see the guide, talking to a pale young fellow in old
corduroy velveteen knee-breeches and an old hat and thick
boots: most obviously German. We go over, make proper
salutes, nod to the German boy, who looks as if he'd had vinegar
for breakfast - and set off. This morning we are going out a
couple of miles, to the farthest end of the necropolis. We have
still a dozen tombs to look at. In all, there are either twenty-five
or twenty-seven painted tombs one can visit[1].

This morning there is a stiff breeze from the south-west. But
it is blowing fresh and clear, not behaving in the ugly way the
libeccio can behave. We march briskly along the highway, the
old dog trundling behind. He loves spending a morning among
the tombs. The sea gives off a certain clearness, that makes the
atmosphere doubly brilliant and exhilarating, as if we were on a
mountain-top. The omnibus rolls by, from Viterbo. In the fields
the peasants are working, and the guide occasionally greets the
women, who give him a sally back again. The young German
tramps firmly on: but his spirit is not as firm as his tread. One
doesn't know what to say to him, he vouchsafes nothing, seems
as if he didn't want to be spoken to, and yet is probably offended
that we don't talk to him. The guide chatters to him in unfailing
cheerfulness, in Italian: but after a while drops back with evident
relief to the milder company of Brewster, leaving me to the
young German, who has certainly swallowed vinegar some time
or other.

But I feel with him as with most of the young people of
today: he has been sinned against more than he sins. The vinegar
was given him to drink. Breaking reluctantly into German, since
Italian seems foolish, and he won't come out in English, I find,
within the first half-mile, that he is twenty-three (he looks
nineteen), has finished his university course, is going to be an

---

[1] The tombs are by now about twice as many but only a few, even only 4 at any one
time, are open to the public.

archaeologist, is travelling doing archaeology, has been in Sicily and Tunis, whence he has just returned; didn't think much of either place - *mehr Schrei wie Wert*, he jerks out, speaking as if he were throwing his words away like a cigarette-end he was sick of; doesn't think much of any place; doesn't think much of the Etruscans - *nicht viel Wert*; doesn't, apparently, think much of me; knows a professor or two whom I have met; knows the tombs of Tarquinia very well, having been here, and stayed here, twice before; doesn't think much of them; he is going to Greece; doesn't expect to think much of it; is staying in the other hotel, not Gentile's, because it is still cheaper: is probably staying a fortnight, going to photograph all the tombs, with a big photographic apparatus - has the Government authority, like the Japs - apparently has very little money indeed, marvellously doing everything on nothing - expects to be a famous professor in a science he doesn't think much of - and I wonder if he always has enough to eat.

He certainly is a fretful and peevish, even if in some ways silent and stoical, young man. *Nicht viel Wert!* - not much worth - doesn't amount to anything - seems to be his favourite phrase, as it is the favourite phrase of almost all young people today. Nothing amounts to anything, for the young.

Well, I feel it's not my fault, and try to bear up. But though it is bad enough to have been of the war generation, it must be worse to have grown up just after the war. One can't blame the young, that they don't find that anything amounts to anything. The war cancelled most meanings for them.

And my young man is not really so bad: he would even rather like to be *made* to believe in something. There is a yearning pathos in him somewhere.

We have passed the modern cemetery, with its white marble headstones, and the arches of a medieval aqueduct mysteriously spanning a dip, and left the high-road, following a path along the long hill-crest, through the green wheat that flutters and ripples in the sea-wind like fine feathers, in the wonderful brilliance of morning. Here and there are tassels of mauve anemones, bits of verbena, many daisies, tufts of camomile. On a rocky mound, which was once a tumulus, the asphodels have the advantage, and send up their spikes on the bright, fresh air, like soldiers clustered on the mount. And we go along this vivid green headland of wheat - which still is rough and uneven, because it was once all tumuli - with our faces to the breeze, the sea-brightness filling the air with exhilaration, and all the country still and silent, and we talk German in the wary way of two dogs sniffing at one another.

Till suddenly we turn off to an almost hidden tomb - the German boy knows the way perfectly. The guide hurries up and lights the acetylene lamp, the dog slowly finds himself a place out of the wind, and flings himself down: and we sink slowly again into the Etruscan world, out of the present world, as we descend underground.

One of the famous tombs at this far-off end of the necropolis is the *Tomb of the Bulls*. It contains what the guide calls: *un po' di pornografico!* - but a very little. The German boy shrugs his 32 shoulders as usual but he informs us that this is one of the oldest tombs of all, and I believe him, for it looks so to me.

It is a little wider than some tombs, the roof has not much pitch, there is a stone bed for sarcophagi along the side walls, and in the end wall are two doorways, cut out of the rock of the end and opening into a second chamber, which seems darker and more dismal. The German boy says this second chamber was cut out later, from the first one. It has no paintings of any importance.

We return to the first chamber, the old one. It is called the Tomb of the Bulls from the two bulls above the doorways of the end of the wall, one a man-faced bull charging at the *'po' di pornografico'*, the other lying down serenely and looking with 33 mysterious eyes into the room, his back turned calmly to the second bit of a picture which the guide says is not *'pornografico'* - «because it is a woman.» The young German smiles with his sour-water expression.

Everything in this tomb suggests the old East: Cyprus, or the Hittites, or the culture of Minos of Crete. Between the doorway of the end wall is a charming painting of a naked horseman with 34 a spear, on a naked horse, moving towards a charming little palm-tree and a well-head or fountain-head, on which repose two sculptured, black-faced beasts, lions with queer black faces. From the mouth of the one near the palm-tree water pours down into a sort of altar-bowl, while on the far side a warrior advances, wearing a bronze helmet and shin-greaves, and apparently menacing the horseman with a sword which he brandishes in his left hand, as he steps up on to the base of the well-head. Both warrior and horseman wear the long, pointed boots of the East: and the palm-tree is not very Italian.

I said to the German: «What do you think it means?» «Ach, nothing! The man on the horse has come to the drinking-trough to water his horse: no more!» And the man with the sword? «Oh, he is perhaps his enemy.» «And the black-faced lions?» «Ach, nothing! Decorations of the fountain.» Below the picture are trees on which hang a garland and a neck-band. The border pattern, instead of the egg and dart, has the sign of Venus, so called, between the darts: a ball surmounted by a little cross. «And that, is that a symbol?» I asked the German. «Here no!» he replied abruptly. «Merely a decoration!» - which is perhaps true. But that the Etruscan artist had no more feeling for it, as a symbol, than a modern house-decorator would have, that we cannot believe.

I gave up for the moment. Above the picture is a sentence lightly written, almost scribbled, in Etruscan. «Can you read it?» I said to the German boy. He read it off quickly - myself, I should have had to go letter by letter. «Do you know what it means?» I asked him. He shrugged his shoulders. «Nobody knows.»

In the shallow angle of the roof the heraldic beasts are curious. The squat centre-piece, the so-called altar, has four rams' heads at the corners. On the right a pale-bodied man with a dark face is galloping up with loose rein, on a black horse, followed by a galloping bull. On the left is a bigger figure, a queer galloping lion with his tongue out. But from the lion's shoulders, instead of wings, rises the second neck of a dark-faced, bearded goat: so that the complex animal has a second, backward-leaning neck and head, of a goat, as well as the first maned neck and menacing head of a lion. The tail of the lion ends in a serpent's head. So this is the proper Chimaera. And galloping after the end of the lion's tail comes a winged female sphinx.

«What is the meaning of this lion with the second head and neck?» I asked the German. He shrugged his shoulders, and said: «Nothing!» It meant nothing to him, because nothing except the ABC of facts means anything to him. He is a scientist, and when he doesn't want a thing to have a meaning it is, *ipso facto,* meaningless.

But the lion with the goat's head springing backwards from its shoulders must mean something, because there it is, very vivid, in the famous bronze *Chimaera of Arezzo*, which is in the 35 Florence museum, and which Benvenuto Cellini restored, and which is one of the most fascinating bronzes in the world. There, the bearded goat's head springs twisting backwards from the lion's shoulders, while the right horn of the goat is seized in the mouth of the serpent, which is the tail of the lion whipped forward over his back.

Though this is the correct Chimaera, with the wounds of Bellerophon in hip and neck, still it is not merely a big toy. It has, and was intended to have, an exact esoteric meaning. In fact, Greek myths are only gross representations of certain very clear and very ancient esoteric conceptions, that are much older than the myths: or the Greeks. Myths, and personal gods, are only the decadence of a previous cosmic religion.

The strange potency and beauty of these Etruscan things arise, it seems to me, from the profundity of the symbolic meaning the artist was more or less aware of. The Etruscan religion, surely, was never anthropomorphic: that is, whatever gods it contained were not *beings*, but symbols of elemental powers, just symbols: as was the case earlier in Egypt. The undivided Godhead, if we can call it such, was symbolised by the *mundum*[2], the plasm-cell with its nucleus: that which is the very beginning; instead of, as with us, by a personal god, a person being the very end of all creation or evolution. So it is all the way through: the Etruscan religion is concerned with all those

[2] See note 6 ch.2.

physical and creative powers and forces which go to the building
up and the destroying of the soul: the soul, the personality, being
that which gradually is produced out of chaos, like a flower,
only to disappear again into chaos, or the underworld. We, on
the contrary, say: In the beginning was the Word! - and deny the
physical universe true existence. We exist only in the Word,
which is beaten out thin to cover, gild, and hide all things.

The human being, to the Etruscan, was a bull or a ram, a
lion or a deer, according to his different aspects and potencies.
The human being had in his veins the blood of the wings of birds
and the venom of serpents. All things emerged from the blood-
stream, and the blood-relation, however complex and contradictory it might become, was never interrupted or forgotten. There
were different currents in the blood-stream, and some always
clashed: bird and serpent, lion and deer, leopard and lamb. Yet
the very clash was a form of unison, as we see in the lion which
also has a goat's head.

But the young German will have nothing of this. He is a
modern, and the obvious alone has true existence for him. A lion
with a goat's head as well as its own head is unthinkable. That
which is unthinkable is non-existent, is nothing. So, all the
Etruscan symbols are to him non-existent and mere crude
incapacity to think. He wastes not a thought on them: they are
spawn of mental impotence, hence negligible.

But perhaps also he doesn't want to give himself away, or
divulge any secret that is going to make him a famous
archaeologist later on. Though I don't think that was it. He was
very nice, showing me details, with his flashlight, that I should
have overlooked. The white horse, for example, has had its
drawing most plainly altered: you can see the old outline of the
horse's back legs and breast, and of the foot of the rider, and you
can see how considerably the artist changed the drawing,
sometimes more than once. He seems to have drawn the whole
thing complete, each time, then changed the position, changed
the direction, to please his feeling. And as there was no
indiarubber to rub out the first attempts, there they are, from at
least six hundred years before Christ: the delicate mistakes of an
Etruscan who had the instinct of a pure artist in him, as well as

the blithe insouciance which makes him leave his alterations for anyone to spy out, if they want to.

The Etruscan artist either drew with the brush or scratched, perhaps, with a nail, the whole outline of their figures on the soft stucco, and then applied their colour *al fresco* . So they had to work quickly. Some of the paintings seemed to me tempera, and in one tomb, I think the *Francesca Giustiniani*, the painting seemed to be done on the naked, creamy rock. In that case, the blue colour of the man's scarf is marvellously vivid.

The subtlety of Etruscan painting, as of Chinese and Hindu, lies in the wonderfully suggestive *edge* of the figures. It is not outlined. It is not what we call 'drawing'. It is the flowing contour where the body suddenly leaves off, upon the atmosphere. The Etruscan artist seems to have seen living things surging from their own centre to their own surface. And the curving and the contour of the silhouette-edge suggests the whole movement of the modelling within. There is actually no modelling. The figures are painted in the flat. Yet they seem of a full, almost turgid muscularity. It is only when we come to the late Tomb of Typhon that we have the figure *modelled*, Pompeian style, with light and shade.

It must have been a wonderful world, that old world where everything appeared alive and shining in the dusk of contact with all things, not merely an isolated individual thing played upon the daylight; where each thing had a clear outline, visually, but in its very clarity was related emotionally or vitally to strange other things, one thing springing from another, things mentally contradictory fusing together emotionally, so that a lion could be at the same moment also a goat, and not a goat. In those days, a man riding on a red horse was not just Jack Smith on his brown nag; it was a suave-skinned creature, with death or life in its face, surging along on a surge of animal power that burned with travel, with the passionate movement of the blood, and which was swirling along on a mysterious course, to some unknown goal, swirling with a weight of its own. Then also, a bull was not merely a stud animal worth so much, due to go to the butcher in a little while. It was a vast wonder-beast, a well-head of the great, furnace-like passion that makes the worlds roll and the sun surge up, and makes a man surge with procreative force; the bull, the herd-lord, the father of calves and heifers, of cows; the father of milk; he who has the horns of power on his forehead, symbolising the warlike aspect of the horn of fertility; the bellowing master of force, jealous, horned, charging against opposition. The goat was in the same line, father of milk, but instead of huge force he had cunning, the cunning *consciousness* and self-consciousness of the jealous, hard-headed father of procreation. Whereas the lion was most terrible, yellow and roaring with a blood-drinking energy, again like the sun, but the sun asserting himself in drinking up the life of the earth. For the sun can warm the worlds, like a yellow hen sitting on her eggs. Or the sun can lick up the life of the world with a hot tongue. The goat says: let me breed for ever, till the world is one reeking goat. But then the lion roars from the other blood-stream, which is also in man, and he lifts his paw to strike, in the passion of the other wisdom.

So all creatures are potential in their own way, a myriad manifold consciousness storming with contradictions and oppositions that are eternal, beyond all mental reconciliation. We can know the living world only symbolically. Yet every consciousness, the rage of the lion, and the venom of the snake, *is*, and therefore is divine. All emerges out of the unbroken circle with its nucleus, the germ, the One, the god, if you like to call it so. And man, with his soul and his personality, emerges in eternal connection with all the rest. The blood-stream is one, and unbroken, yet storming with oppositions and contradictions.

The ancients saw, consciously, as children now see unconsciously, the everlasting *wonder* in things. In the ancient world the three compelling emotions must have been emotions of wonder, fear and admiration: admiration in the Latin sense of the world, as well as our sense; and fear in its largest meaning, including repulsion, dread and hate: then arose the last, individual emotion of pride. Love is only a subsidiary factor in wonder and admiration.

But it was by seeing all things alert in the throb of interrelated passional significance that the ancients kept the wonder and the delight in life, as well as the dread and the repugnance. They were like children: but they had force, the power and the sensual *knowledge* of true adults. They had a world of valuable knowledge, which is utterly lost to us. Where they were true adults, we are children; and vice versa.

Even the two bits of *'pornografico'* in the Tomb of the Bull are not two little dirty drawings. Far from it. The German boy felt this, as we did. The drawings have the same naïve wonder in them as the rest, the same archaic innocence, accepting life, knowing all about it, and *feeling* the meaning, which is like a stone fallen into consciousness, sending its rings ebbing out and out, to the extremes. The two little pictures have a symbolic meaning, quite distinct from a *moral* meaning - or an immoral. The words moral and immoral have no force. Some acts - what Dennis would call flagrant obscenity - the man-faced bull accepts calmly lying down; against other acts he charges with lowered horns. It is not judgement. It is the sway of passional action and reaction: the action and reaction of the father of milk.

There are beautiful tombs, in this far-off wheat-covered hill. The *Tomb of the Augurs* is very impressive. On the end wall is painted a doorway to a tomb, and on either side of it is a man 37
making what is probably the morning gesture, strange and momentous, one hand to the brow. The two men are mourning at the door of the tomb.

«No!» says the German. «The painted door does not represent the door to the tomb, with mourners on either side. It is merely the painted door which later they intended to cut out, to make a second chamber to the tomb. And the men are not mourning.»

«Then what are they doing?»

Shrug!

In the triangle above the painted door two lions, a white-faced one and a dark-faced, have seized a goat or an antelope: the dark-faced lion turns over and bites the side of the goat's neck, the white-faced bites the haunch. Here we have again the two heraldic beasts: but instead of their roaring at the altar, or the tree, they are biting the goat, the father of milk-giving life, in throat and hip.

On the side walls are very fine frescoes of nude wrestlers,

and then of a scene which has started a lot of talk about
38 Etruscan cruelty. A man with his head in a sack, wearing only a
    skin-girdle, is being bitten in the thigh by a fierce dog which is
39 held, by another man, on a string attached to what is apparently
    a wooden leash, this wooden handle being fastened to the dog's
    collar. The man who holds the string wears a peculiar high
    conical hat, and he stands, big-limbed and excited, striding
    behind the man with his head in the sack. This victim is by now
    getting entangled in the string, the long, long cord which holds
    the dog; but with his left hand he seems to be getting hold of the
    cord to drag the dog off from his thigh, while in his right hand
    he holds a huge club, with which to strike the dog when he can
    get it into striking range.

    This picture is supposed to reveal the barbarously cruel
    sports of the Etruscans. But since the tomb contains an augur,
    with his curved sceptre, tensely lifting his hand to the dark bird
    that flies by: and the wrestlers are wrestling over a curious pile of
    three great bowls; and on the other side of the tomb the man in
    the conical pointed hat, he who holds the string in the first
    picture, is now dancing with a peculiar delight, as if rejoicing in
    victory or liberation[3]: we must surely consider this picture as
    symbolic, along with all the rest: the fight of the blindfolded man
    with some raging, attacking element. If it were sport there would
    be onlookers, as there are at the sports in the *Tomb of the
    Chariots*; and here there are none.

    However, the scenes portrayed in the tomb are all so real,
    that it seems they must have taken place in actual life. Perhaps
    there was some form of test or trial which gave a man a great
    club, tied his head in a sack, and left him to fight a fierce dog
    which attacked him, but which was held on a string, and which
    even had a wooden grip-handle attached to its collar, by which
    the man might seize it and hold it firm, while he knocked it on
    the head. The man in the sack has very good chances against the
    dog. And even granted the thing was done for sport, and not as
    some sort of trial or test, the cruelty is not excessive, for the man
    has a very good chance of knocking the dog on the head quite

    ---

    [3] It's the character portrayed in the embroidery worked in wool by Frieda Lawrence
    upon an original sketch by L., reproduced on the front cover.

early. Compared with Roman gladiatorial shows, it is almost
'fair play'.

But it must be more than sport. The dancing of the man who
held the string is too splendid. And the tomb is, somehow, too
intense, too meaningful. And the dog - or wolf or lion - that bites
the thigh of the man is too old a symbol. We have it very plainly
on the top of the *Sarcophagus of the Painted Amazons*, in the 40
Florence museum. This sarcophagus comes from Tarquinia - and
the end of the lid has a carved naked man, with legs apart, a dog
on each side biting him in the thigh. They are the dogs of disease
and death, biting at the great arteries of the thigh, where the
elementary life surges in a man. The motive is common in
ancient symbolism. And the esoteric idea of malevolent influences attacking the great arteries of the thighs was turned in Greece
into the myth of Actaeon and his dogs.

Another fine tomb is the *Tomb of the Baron*, with its frieze 41
of single figures, dark on a light background going round the
walls. There are horses and men, all in dark silhouette, and very
fascinating in drawing. These archaic horses are so perfectly
satisfying *as* horses: so far more horselike, to the soul, than those
of Rosa Bonheur or Rubens or even Velazquez, though he comes
nearer to these: so that one asks oneself, what, after all, is the
horsiness of a horse? - what is it, that will never be put into
words? For a man who sees, sees not as a camera does when it
takes a snapshot, not even as a cinema-camera, taking its
succession of instantaneous snaps; but in a curious rolling flood
of vision, in which the image itself seethes and rolls; and only the
mind *picks out* certain factors which *shall* represent the image
seen. That is why a camera is so unsatisfactory: its eye is flat, it
is related only to a negative thing inside the box: whereas inside
our living box there is a decided positive.

We go from tomb to tomb, down into the dark, up again
into the wind and the brilliance; and the day rolls by. But we are
moving, tomb by tomb, gradually nearer the city. The new
cemetery draws near. We have passed the aqueduct, which
crosses the dip, then takes an underground channel towards the
town. Near the cemetery we descend into a big tomb, the biggest
we have yet seen - a great underground cavern with great wide

beds for sarcophagi and biers, and in the centre a massive square
pillar or shaft on which is painted a *Typhon* - the seaman with
coiled snake-legs, and wings behind his arms, his hands holding
up the roof; two Typhons, another on the opposite face of the
pillar, almost identical with the first.

In this place, almost at once, the Etruscan charm seems to
vanish. The tomb is big, crude, somehow ugly like a cavern. The
Typhon, with his reddish flesh and light-and-shade modelling, is
clever, and might be modern, done for effect. He is rather
Pompeian - and a little like Blake. But he is done from quite a
new consciousness, external; the old inwardness has gone.
Dennis[4], who saw him eighty years ago, thinks him far more
marvellous than the archaic dancers. But we do not.

There are some curly-wig dolphins sporting over a curly
border which, but for experience, we should not know was the
sea. And there is a border of 'rose', really the sacred symbol of
the 'one' with its central germ, here for the first time vulgarly
used. There is also a fragment of a procession to Hades, which
must have been rather fine in the Graeco-Roman style. But the
true archaic charm is utterly gone. The dancing Etruscan spirit is
dead.

This is one of the very latest tombs: said to be of the second
century B.C., when the Romans had long been masters of
Tarquinia. Veii, the first great Etruscan city to be captured by
Rome, was taken about 388 B.C., and completely destroyed.
From then on, Etruria gradually weakened and sank, till the
peace of 280 B.C., when we may say the military conquest of
Etruria was complete.

So that the tombs suddenly change. Those supposed to be of
the fifth century, like the Tomb of the Baron, with the frieze of
horses and men, or the Tomb of the Leopards, are still perfectly
Etruscan, no matter what touch of Orient they may have, and
perfectly charming. Then suddenly we come to the *Tomb of the
Orcus*, or Hell, which is given the fourth century as a date, and
here the whole thing utterly changes. You get a great gloomy,
clumsy, rambling sort of underworld, damp and horrid, with
large but much-damaged pictures on the walls.

---

[4] See Dennis 1883; I, 327 ff.

These paintings, though they are interesting in their way, and have scribbled Etruscan inscriptions, have suddenly lost all Etruscan charm. They still have a bit of Etruscan freedom, but on the whole they are Graeco-Roman, half suggesting Pompeian, half suggesting Roman things. They are more free than the paintings of the little old tombs; at the same time, all the motion is gone; the figures are stuck there without any vital flow between them. There is no touch.

Instead of the wonderful old silhouette forms we have modern 'drawing', often quite good. But to me it is an intense disappointment.

When the Romans took the power from the hands of the Etruscan Lucumones - in the fourth century B.C. - and made them merely Roman magistrates, at the best, the mystery of Etruria died almost at once. In the ancient world of king-gods, governing according to a religious conception, the deposition of the chiefs and the leading priests leaves the country at once voiceless and mindless. So it was in Egypt and Babylonia, in Assyria, in the Aztec and Maya lordships of America. The people are governed by the flower of the race. Pluck the flower and the race is helpless.

The Etruscans were not destroyed. But they lost their being. They had lived, ultimately, by the *subjective* control of the great natural powers. Their subjective power fell before the objective power of the Romans. And almost at once the true race-consciousness finished. The Etruscan knowledge became mere superstition. The Etruscan princes became fat and inert Romans. The Etruscan people became expressionless and meaningless. It happened amazingly quickly, in the third and second centuries B.C.

Yet the Etruscan *blood* continued to beat. And Giotto[5] and

---

[5] The idea must be certainly ascribed to John Ruskin (1819- 1900): «You will also please take it on my word to day that Giotto was a pure Etruscan-Greek of the thirteeenth century: converted indeed to worship St. Francis instead of Heracles; but as far as vase-painting, precisely the Etruscan he was before. ... Etruscan art remains in its own Italian valleys, of the Arno and Upper Tiber, in one unbroken series of work, from the seventh century before Christ, to this hour, when the country whitewasher still scratches its plaster in Etruscan patterns. All Florentine work of the finest kind - Luca della Robbia's, Ghiberti's, Donatello's, Filippo Lippi's, Botticelli's, Fra Angelico's - is absolutely pure Etruscan, merely changing its subjects, and representing the Virgin

the early sculptors seem to have been a flowering again of the Etruscan blood, which is always putting forth a flower, and always being trodden down again by some superior 'force'. It is a struggle between the endless patience of life and the endless triumph of force.

There is one other huge late tomb, the *Tomb of the Shields*, 44 said to be of the third century. It contains many fragmentary paintings. There is a banqueting scene, with a man on the banqueting bench taking the egg from the woman, and she is touching his shoulder. But they might as well be two chairs from a 'suite'. There is nothing between them. And they have those 'important' sort of faces - all outside, nothing inside - that are so boring. Yet they are interesting. They might almost be done today, by an ultra-modern artist bent on being absolutely child-like and naïve and archaic. But after the real archaic paintings, these are empty. The air is empty. The egg is still held up. But it means no more to that man and woman than the chocolate Easter egg does to us. It has gone cold.

In the Tomb of Orcus begins the representation of the grisly underworld, hell and its horrors, which surely was reflected on to the Etruscans from the grisly Romans. The lovely little tombs of just one small chamber, or perhaps two chambers, of the earlier centuries give way to these great sinister caverns underground, and hell is fitly introduced.

The old religion of the profound attempt of man to harmonise himself with nature, and hold his own and come to flower in the great seething of life, changed with the Greeks and Romans into a desire to resist nature, to produce a mental cunning and a mechanical force that would outwit Nature and chain her down completely, completely, till at last there should be nothing free in nature at all, all should be controlled, domesticated, put to man's meaner uses. Curiously enough, with the idea of the triumph over nature arose the idea of a gloomy Hades, a hell and purgatory. To the peoples of the Idea the after-life is hell, or nothingness, and paradise is an inadequate fiction.

But, naturally enough, historians seized on these essentially

instead of Athena, and Christ instead of Jupiter».(*Mornings in Florence* Orpington, 1881 ed. 1907, 90-91).

non-Etruscan evidences, in the Etruscan late tombs, to build up a picture of a gloomy, hellish, serpent-writhing, vicious Etruscan people who were quite rightly stamped out by the noble Romans. This myth is still not dead. Men *never* want to believe the evidence of their senses. They would far rather go on elaborating some 'classical' author. The whole science of history seems to be the picking of old fables and old lies into fine threads, and wearing them up again. Theopompus[6] collected some scandalous tales, and that is quite enough. The evidence of fifty million gay little tombs wouldn't weigh a straw. In the beginning was the Word, indeed! Even the word of a Theopompus!

Perhaps the favourite painting for representing the beauties of the Etruscan tombs is the well-known head of a woman, seen in profile with wheat-ears for a head-wreath, or fillet. This head comes from the Tomb of Orcus, and is chosen because it is far more Greek-Roman than it is Etruscan. As a matter of fact, it is rather stupid and self-conscious - and modern. But it belongs to the classic Convention, and men can only see according to a Convention. We haven't exactly plucked our eyes out, but we've plucked out three-fourths of their vision.

After the Tomb of the Typhon one has had enough. There is nothing really Etruscan left. It is better to abandon the necropolis altogether, and to remember that almost everything we know of the Etruscans from the classic authors is comparable to the paintings in the late tombs. It refers only to the fallen, Romanised Etruscans of the decadence.

It is very pleasant to go down from the hill on which the present Tarquinia stands, down into the valley and up to the

45

---

[6] Theopompus' opinion is recorded in a passage of the *Deipnosophistai* (XII; 517d - 518a) of Athenaeus of Naucrates (III C. B.C.). Athenaeus writes: «Theopompus, in Book 43 of the *Phillippian History* tells us that among the Etruscans there is a law according to which all women are in common. These women have great care of their bodies, and often strip off in the presence of men, or even amid me, for among them it is not obscene to show oneself in the nude. Then they sit at banquet, but not with their spouses, but with whomever might be present, and they do easily give in to anybody they might feel inclined towards. They are also resistant in drinking, and very fair looking. The Etruscans feed all children that are born, ignoring their paternity.» Ducati (1925; I 170-72) comments that these are just «exaggeration of the great importance of women in Etruscan society».

opposite hill, on which the Etruscan Tarquinii surely stood. There are many flowers, the blue grape-hyacinth and the white, the mauve tassel anemone, and, in a corner of a field of wheat, the big purple anemone, then a patch of the big pale pink anemone with the red, sore centre - the big-petalled sort. It is curious how the anemone varies. Only in this one place in Tarquinia have I found the whity-pink kind, with the dark, sore-red centre. But probably that is just chance.

The town ends really with the wall. At the foot of the wall is
46 wild hillside, and down the slope is only one little farm, with another little house made of straw. The country is clear of houses. The peasants live in the city.

Probably in Etruscan days it was much the same, but there must have been far more people on the land, and probably there were many little straw huts, little temporary houses, among the green corn: and fine roads, such as the Etruscans taught the Romans to build, went between the hills: and the high black walls, with towers, wound along the hill-crest.

The Etruscans, though they grew rich as traders and metal-workers, seem to have lived chiefly by the land. The intense culture of the land by the Italian peasant of today seems like the remains of the Etruscan system. On the other hand, it was Roman, and not Etruscan, to have large villas in the country, with the great compound or 'factory' for the slaves, who were shut in at night, and in a gang taken out to labour during the day. The huge farms of Sicily and Lombardy and others parts of Italy must be remains of this Roman system: the big *fattorie*. But one imagines the Etruscans had a different system: that the peasants were serfs rather than slaves: that they had their own small portions of land, which they worked to full pitch, from father to son, giving a portion of the produce to the masters, keeping a portion for themselves. So they were half-free, at least, and had a true life of their own, stimulated by the religious life of their masters.

The Romans changed it all. They did not like the country. In palmy days they built great villas with barracks for slaves, out in the country. But, even so, it was easier to get rich by commerce or conquest. So the Romans gradually abandoned the land, which fell into neglect and prepared the way for the Dark Ages.

The wind blows stiffer and stiffer from the south-west. There are no trees: but even the bushes bend away from it. And when we get to the crown of the long, lonely hill on which stood the Etruscan Tarquinii we are almost blown from our feet, and have to sit down behind a thicket of bushes for a moment's shelter, to watch the great black-and-white cattle stepping slowly down to the drinking-place, the young bulls curving and playing. 52 All along the hilltop the green wheat ruffles like soft hair. Away inland the green land looks empty, save for a far-off town perched on a hill-top, like a vision. On the next hill, towards the sea, Tarquinia holds up her square towers, in vain.

And we are sitting on what would be the arx of the vanished city. Somewhere here the augurs held up their curved staffs, and watched the birds move across the quarters of the city. We can do so much even today. But of the city I cannot find even one stone[7]. It is so lonely and open.

One can go back up a different road, and in through another gate of the city today. We drop quickly down, in the fierce wind, down to calm. The road winds up slowly from the little valley, but we are in shelter from the wind. So we pass the first wall, through the first medieval gateway. The road winds inside the wall, past the *Dazio,* but there are no houses. A bunch of men are excitedly playing *morra*, and the shouts of the numbers come 48 up like explosions, with wild excitement. The men glance at us apprehensively, but laugh as we laugh.

So we pass on through a second frowning gateway, inside the second circle of walls. And still we are not in the town. There is still a third wall, and a third massive gate. And then we are in 47 the old part of the town, where the graceful little palazzos of the Middle Ages are turned into stables and barns, and into houses for poor peasants. In front of the lower storey of one little old palace, now a blacksmith's shop, the smith is shoeing a refractory mule, which kicks and plunges, and brings loud

---

[7] The excavations intended to bring to light the monumental complex known as the *Ara della Regina,* a great truncated pyramid of square blocks, already known by this name to Dennis (1883; I, 426) were in fact undertaken only in 1948.

shouts from the inevitable little group of onlookers.

Queer and lonely and slummy the waste corners and narrow streets seem, forlorn, as if belonging to another age. On a beautiful stone balcony a bit of poor washing is drying. The houses seem dark and furtive, people lurking like rats. And then again rises another tall, sharp-edged tower, blank and blind. They have a queer effect on a town, these sharp, rigid, blind, meaningless towers, soaring away with their sharp edges into the sky, for no reason, beyond the house-roofs; and from the far distance, when one sees the little city down far off, suggesting the factory chimneys of a modern town.

They are the towers which in the first place were built for retreat and defence, when this coast was ravaged by sea-rovers. Norman adventurers, or Barbary pirates that were such a scourge to the Mediterranean. Later, however, the medieval nobles built towers just for pure swank, to see who should have the tallest, till a town like Bologna must have bristled like a porcupine in a rage, or like Pittsburgh with chimney-stacks - square ones. Then the law forbade towers - and towers, after having scraped the heavens, began to come down. There are some still, however, in Tarquinia, where age overlaps age.

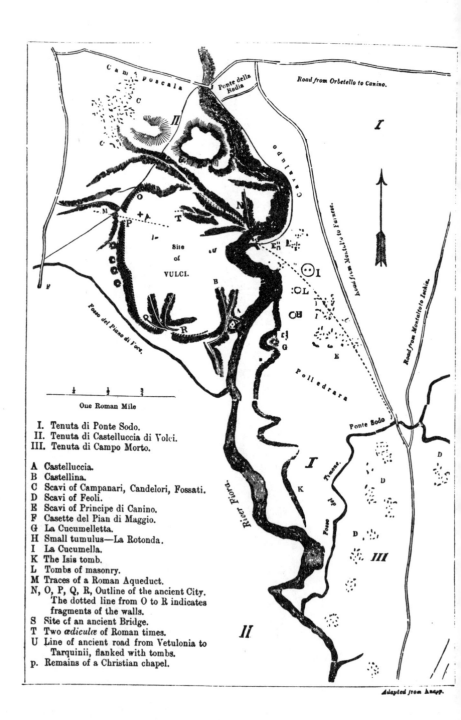

One Roman Mile

I. Tenuta di Ponte Sodo.
II. Tenuta di Castelluccia di Volci.
III. Tenuta di Campo Morto.

A Castelluccia.
B Castellina.
C Scavi of Campanari, Candelori, Fossati.
D Scavi of Feoli.
E Scavi of Principe di Canino.
F Casette del Pian di Maggio.
G La Cucumelletta.
H Small tumulus—La Rotonda.
I La Cucumella.
K The Isis tomb.
L Tombs of masonry.
M Traces of a Roman Aqueduct.
N, O, P, Q, R, Outline of the ancient City.
      The dotted line from O to R indicates
      fragments of the walls.
S Site of an ancient Bridge.
T Two *ædiculæ* of Roman times.
U Line of ancient road from Vetulonia to
      Tarquinii, flanked with tombs.
p. Remains of a Christian chapel.

Adapted from Anayy.

5 - VULCI

Ancient Etruria consisted of a league, or loose religious Confederacy of twelve cities, each city embracing some miles of country all around, so that we may say there were twelve states, twelve city-states, the famous *dodecapolis* of the ancient world, the Latin *duodecim populi Etruriae.* Of these twelve city-states, Tarquinii was supposed to be the oldest, and the chief. Caere is another city: and not far off, to the north, Vulci.

Vulci is now called Volci - though there is no city, only a hunting-ground for treasure in Etruscan tombs. The Etruscan city fell into decay in the decline of the Roman Empire, and either lapsed owing to the malaria which came to fill this region with death, or else was finally wiped out, as Ducati[1] says, by the Saracens. Anyhow there is no life there now.

I asked the German boy about the Etruscan places along the coast: Volci, Vetulonia, Populonia. His answer was always the same: «Nothing! Nothing! There is nothing there!»

However, we determined to look at Volci. It lies only about a dozen miles north of Tarquinia. We took the train, one station only, to Montalto di Castro, and were rattled up to the little town on the hill, not far inland. The morning was still fairly early - and Saturday. But the town, or village, on the hill was very quiet and dead-alive. We got down from the bus in a sort of nowhere-seeming little piazza; the town had no centre of life. But there was a café, so in we went, asked for coffee, and where could we get a carriage to take us to Volci.

The man in the little café was yellow and slow, with the

---

[1] Ducati 1925 II,194.

slow smile of the peasants. He seemed to have no energy at all: and eyed us lethargically. Probably he had malaria - though the fevers were not troubling him at the time. But it had eaten into his life.

He said, did we want to go to the bridge - the *Ponte*? I said yes, the *Ponte dell'Abbadia:* because I knew that Volci was near to this famous old bridge of the monastery. I asked him if we could get a light cart to drive us out. He said it would be difficult. I said, then we could walk: it was only five miles, eight kilometres. «Eight kilometres!» he said, in the slow, laconic malarial fashion, looking at me with a glint of ridicule in his black eyes. «It is at least twelve!»

«The book says eight!» I insisted stoutly. They always want to make distances twice as long, if you are to hire a carriage. But he watched me slowly, and shook his head. «Twelve!» he said. «Then we must have a carriage,» said I. «You wouldn't find your way anyhow,» said the man. «Is there a carriage?» He didn't know. There was one, but it had gone off somewhere this morning, and wouldn't be back till two or three in the afternoon. The usual story.

I insisted, was there no little cart, no *barrocino,* no *carretto*? He slowly shook his head. But I continued to insist, gazing at him fixedly, as if a carriage *must* be produced. So at last we went out, to look. He came back, after a time, shaking his head. Then he had a colloquy with his wife. Then he went out again, and was gone ten minutes.

A dusty little baker, a small man very full of energy, as little Italians often are, came in and asked for a drink. He sat down a minute and drank his drink, eyeing us from his floury face. Then he got up and left the shop again. In a moment the café man returned, and said that perhaps there was a *carretto*. I asked where it was. He said the man was coming.

The drive to the Ponte was apparently two hours - then the trip would be six hours. We should have to take a little food with us - there was nothing there.

A small-faced, weedy sort of youth appeared in the door- way: also malaria! We could have the *carretto*. «For how much?» «Seventy liras!» «Too much!» said I. «Far too much!

Fifty or nothing. Take it or leave it, fifty!» The youth in the
doorway looked blank. The café man, always with his faint little
sardonic smile, told the youth to go and ask. The youth went.
We waited. Then the youth came back, to say all right! So!
«How long?» «*Subito!*» *Subito* means immediately, but it is as well
to be definite. «Ten minutes?» said I. «Perhaps twenty!» said the
youth. «Better say twenty!» said the café man: who was an
honest man, really, and rather pleasant in his silent way.

   We went out to buy a little food, and the café man went with
us. The shops in the place were just holes. We went to the baker.
Outside stood a cart being loaded with bread, by the youth and
the small, quick-silver baker. Inside the shop, we bought a long
loaf, and a few bits of sliced sausage, and asked for cheese.
There was no cheese - but they would get us some. We waited an
infinite while. I said to the café man, who waited alongside, full
of interest: «Won't the *carretto* be ready?» He turned round and
pointed to the tall, randy mare between the shafts of the bread-
cart outside. «That's the horse that will take you. When the
bread is delivered, they will hitch her into the *carretto*, and the
youth will drive you.» There was nothing for it but patience, for
the baker's mare and the baker's youth were our only hope. The
cheese came at last. We wandered out to look for oranges. There
was a woman selling them on a low bench beside the road, but
Brewster, who was getting impatient, didn't like the look of
them. So we went across to a little hole of a shop where another
woman had oranges. They were tiny ones, and Brewster was
rejecting them with impatient scorn. But the woman insisted they
were sweet, sweet as apples, and full of juice. We bought four:
and I bought a *finocchio* for a salad. But she was right. The
oranges were exquisite, when we came to eat them, and we
wished we had ten.

   On the whole, I think the people in Montalto are honest and
rather attractive, but most of them slow and silent. It must be
the malaria every time.

   The café man asked if we would stay the night. We said, was
there an inn? He said: «Oh yes, several!» I asked where, and he
pointed up the street. «But,» said I, «what do you want with
several hotels here?» «For the agents who come to buy agricultu-

ral produce,» he said. «Montalto is the centre of a great agricultural industry, and many agents come, many!» However, I decided that, if we could, we would leave in the evening. There was nothing in Montalto to keep us.

At last the *carretto* was ready: a roomy, two-wheeled gig hung rather low. We got in, behind the dark, mulberry mare, and the baker's youth, who certainly hadn't washed his face for some days, started us on the trip. He was in an agony of shyness, stupefied.

The town is left behind at once. The green land, with squares of leaden-dark olives planted in rows, slopes down to the railway line, which runs along the coast parallel with the ancient Via Aurelia. Beyond the railway is the flatness of the coastal strip, and the whitish emptiness of the sea's edge. It gives a great sense of nothingness, the sea down there.

The mulberry mare, lean and spare, reaches out and makes a good pace. But very soon we leave the road and are on a wide, wide trail of pinkish clayey earth, made up entirely of ruts. In parts the mud is still deep, water stands in the fathomless mud-holes. But, fortunately, for a week it hasn't rained, so the road is passable; most of the ruts are dry, and the wide trail, wide as a desert road which has no confines, is not difficult, only jolty. We run the risk of having our necks jerked out of their sockets by the impatient, long-striding mare.

The boy is getting over his shyness, now he is warmed up to driving, and proves outspoken and straightforward. I said to him: «What a good thing the road is dry!» «If it had been fifteen days ago,» he said, «you couldn't have passed.» But in the late afternoon, when we were returning on the same road and I said: «In bad wet weather we should have to come through here on horseback,» he replied «Even with the *carretto* you can get through.» «Always?» said I. «Always!» said he.

And that was how he was. Possibility or impossibility was just a frame of mind with him.

We were on the Maremma, that flat, wide plain of the coast that has been water-logged for centuries, and one of the most abandoned, wildest parts of Italy. Under the Etruscans, apparently, it was an intensely fertile plain. But the Etruscans seem to have been very clever drainage-engineers; they drained the land so that it was a waving bed of wheat, with their methods of intensive peasant culture. Under the Romans, however, the elaborate system of canals and levels of water fell into decay, and gradually the streams threw their mud along the coast and choked themselves, then soaked into the land and made marshes and vast stagnant shallow pools where the mosquitoes bred like fiends, millions hatching on a warm May day; and with the mosquitoes came the malaria, called the marsh fever in the old days. Already in late Roman times this evil had fallen on the Etruscan plains and on the Campagna of Rome. Then, apparently, the land rose in level, the sea-strip was wider but even more hollow than before, the marshes became deadly, and human life departed or was destroyed, or lingered on here and there.

In Etruscan days, no doubt, large tracts of this coast were covered with pine-forest, as are the slopes of the mountains that rise a few miles inland, and stretches of the coast still, farther north. The pleasant *pineta*, or open, sparse forest of umbrella-pines, once spread on and on, with tall arbutus and heather covering the earth from which the reddish trunks rose singly, as from an endless moor, and tufts of arbutus and broom making thickets. The pine-woods farther north are still delightful, so silent and bosky, with the umbrella roofs.

But the pine will not bear being soaked. So, as the great pools and marshes spread, the trees of Etruscan days fell for ever, and great treeless tracts appeared, covered with an almost impenetrable low jungle of brush and scrub and reeds, spreading for miles, and quite manless. The arbutus, that is always glossy green, and the myrtle, the mastic-tree, heaths, broom, and other spiny, gummy, coarse moorland plants rose up in dense luxuriance, to have their tops bent and whipped off by the ever-whipping winds from the sea, so that there was a low, dark jungle of scrub, less than man-high, stretching in places from the mountains almost to the sea. And here the wild boar roamed in herds; foxes and wolves hunted the rabbits, the hares, the roebuck; the innumerable wild-fowl and the flamingos walked the sickly, stricken shores of the great pools and the sea.

So the Maremma country lay for centuries, with cleared

tracts between, and districts a little elevated, and therefore rich
in produce, but for the most part a wilderness, where the
herdsmen pastured sheep, if possible, and the buffaloes roamed
unherded. In 1828, however, the Grand-Duke Leopold of
Tuscany signed the decree for the reclaiming of the Maremma[2],
and lately the Italian Government has achieved splendid results -
great tracts of farmland added on to the country's resources, and
new farms stuck up.

But still there are large tracts of moorland. We bowled along
the grassy ruts, towards the distant mountains, and first all was
wheat; then it was moorland, with great, grey-headed carrion-
crow floating around in the bareness; then a little thicket of ilex-
oak; then another patch of wheat; and then a desolate sort of
farmhouse, that somehow reminded one of America, a rather
dismal farm on the naked prairie, all alone.

The youth told me he had been for two years *guardiano*, or
herdsman, at this place. The large cattle were lingering around
the naked house, within the wire enclosure. But there was a
notice that the place was shut off, because of foot-and-mouth
disease. The driver saluted a dismal woman and two children as
he drove by.

We made a good pace. The driver, Luigi, told me his father
had been also a *guardiano*, a herdsman, in this district, his five
sons following him. The youth would look round, into the
distance, with that keen, far-off look of men who have always
lived wild and apart, and who are in their own country. He
knew every sign. And he was so glad to get out again, out of
Montalto.

The father, however, had died, a brother had married and
lived in the family house, and Luigi had gone to help the baker in
Montalto. But he was not happy: caged. He revived and became
alert once more out in the Maremma spaces. He had lived more
or less alone all his life - he was only eighteen - and loneliness,
space, was precious to him, as it is to a moorland bird.

The great hooded crows floated round, and many big

---

[2] Leopold's project of reclamation, based on the assumption that it was the
'admixture of fresh and salty waters' to cause malaria was only moderately successful,
and caused a large number of victims among the navvies.

meadow-larks rose up from the moor. Save for this, everything to us was silent. Luigi said that now the hunting season was closed: but still, if he had a gun, he could take a shot at those hooded crows. It was obvious he was accustomed to have a gun in his hand when he was out in the long, hot, malarial days, mounted on a pony, watching the herds of cattle roving on the Maremma. Cattle do not take malaria.

I asked him about game. He said there was much in the foothills there. And he pointed away ahead, to where the mountains began to rise, six or eight miles away. Now so much of the Maremma itself is drained and cleared, the game is in the hills. His father used to accompany the hunters in winter: they still arrive in winter-time, the hunters in their hunting outfit, with dogs, and a great deal of fuss and paraphernalia, from Rome or from Florence. And still they catch the wild boar, the fox, the *capriolo*: which I suppose means the roedeer rather than the wild goat. But the boar is the *pièce de resistance*. You may ⁵³ see his bristling carcass in the market-place in Florence, now and again, in winter. But, like every other wild thing on earth, he is becoming scarcer and scarcer. Soon the only animals left will be tame ones: man the tamest and most swarming. Adieu even to Maremma.

«There!» said the boy. «There is the bridge of the monastery!» We looked into the shallow hollow of green land, and could just see a little, black sort of tower by some bushes, in the empty landscape. There was a long, straight ditch or canal, and digging evidently going on. It was the Government irrigation works.

We left the road and went bowling over rough grass, by tracts of poor-looking oats. Luigi said they would cut these oats for fodder. There was a scrap of a herdsman's house, and new wire fences along the embankment of the big irrigation canal. This was new to Luigi. He turned the mare uphill again, towards the house, and asked the urchin where he was to get through the wire fence. The urchin explained - Luigi had it in a moment. He was intelligent as a wild thing, out here in his own spaces.

«Five years ago,» he said, «there was none of this» - and he pointed around. «No canal, no fences, no oats, no wheat. It was all *maremma*, moorland, with no life save the hooded crows, the cattle and the herdsmen. Now the cattle are all going - the herds are only remnants. And the ranch-houses are being abandoned.» He pointed away to a large house some miles off, on the nearest hill-foot. «There, there are no more cattle, no more herdsmen.

51 The steam-plough comes and ploughs the earth, the machinery sows and reaps the wheat and oats, the people of the Maremma, instead of being more, are fewer. The wheat grows by machinery.»

We were on a sort of trail again, bowling down a slight incline towards a bushy hollow and a black old ruin with a tower. Soon we saw that in the hollow was a tree-filled ravine,

54 quite deep. And over the ravine a queer bridge, curving up like a rainbow, and narrow and steep and fortified-seeming. It soared over the ravine in one high curve, the stony path nipped in like a gutter between its broken walls, and charging straight at the black lava front of the ruin opposite, which was once a castle of the frontier. The little river in the gully, the Fiora, formed the boundary between the Papal States and Tuscany, so the castle guarded the bridge.

We wanted to get down, but Luigi made us wait, while he ran ahead to negotiate. He came back, climbed in, and drove up between the walls of the bridge. It was just wide enough for the cart: just. The walls of the bridge seemed to touch us. It was like climbing up a sort of gutter. Far below, way down in a thicket of bushes, the river rushed - the Fiora, a mere torrent or rain-stream.

We drove over the bridge, and at the far end the lava wall of the monastery seemed to shut us back, the mare's nose almost touched it. The road, however, turned to the left under an arched gateway. Luigi edged the mare round cleverly. There was just room to get her round with the *carretto*, out of the mouth of the bridge and under the archway, scraping the wall of the castle.

So! We were through. We drove a few yards past the ruin, and got down on a grassy place over the ravine. It was a wonderfully romantic spot. The ancient bridge, built in the first place by the Etruscans of Vulci, of blocks of black *tufo*, goes up in the air like a black bubble, so round and strange. The little river is in the bushy cleft, a hundred feet below. The bridge is in the sky, like a black bubble, most strange and lonely, with the poignancy of perfect things long forgotten. It has, of course, been restored in Roman and medieval days. But essentially it is Etruscan, a beautiful Etruscan movement.

Pressing on to it, on this side, is the black building of the castle, mostly in ruins, with grass growing from the tops of the walls and from the black tower. Like the bridge, it is built of blocks of reddish black, spongy lava-stone, but its blocks are much squarer.

And all around is a peculiar emptiness. The castle is not entirely ruined. It is a sort of peasant farmstead. Luigi knows the people who live there. And across the stream there are patches of oats, and two or three cattle feeding, and two children. But all on this side, towards the mountains, is heathy, waste moorland, over which the trail goes towards the hills, and towards a great house among trees which we had seen from the distance. That is the *Badia*, or monastery, which gave the name to the bridge. But it has long been turned into a villa. The whole of this property belonged to Lucien Bonaparte, Prince of Canino, brother of Napoleon. He lived here after the death of his brother, as an Italian prince[3]. In 1828 some oxen ploughing the land near the castle suddenly went through the surface of the earth, and sank into a tomb, in which were broken vases. This at once led to excavations. It was the time when the «Grecian urn» was most popular. Lucien Bonaparte had no interest in vases. He hired an overseer to superintend the excavating, giving orders that every painted fragment must be saved, but that coarse ware must be smashed, to prevent the cheapening of the market. So that the work went savagely on, vases and basketfuls of broken pieces were harvested, the coarse, rough black Etruscan ware was smashed to pieces, as it was discovered, the overseer guarding

[3] Lucien Bonaparte (b. Ajaccio 1775 - d. Viterbo 1840) in 1802 clashed with his brother over his marriage with a divorcee, and took refuge in the Papal States, where in 1814 Pius VII bestowed on him the title of Prince of Canino. Having come to terms with Napoleon during the latter 'One-Hundred Days' on Elba, in his later years Lucien kept busy excavating his lands, writing novels and poems (*Tribu indienne ou Eduard et Stelline* in 2 vols. Paris, 1799; *Charlemagne ou l'Eglise sauvee* in 24 cantos Rome, 1814), besides his troublesome attempts to reorganize the Bonapartist party.

the workmen with his gun over his knees. Dennis saw this still
happening in 1846, when Lucien was dead. But the work was
still going on, under the Princess's charge. And vainly Dennis
asked the overseer to spare him some of the rough black ware.
Not one! Smash they went to earth, while the overseer sat with
his gun over his knees ready to shoot. But the bits of painted
pottery were most skilfully fitted together, by the Princess's
expert workmen, and she would sell some patera or amphora for
a thousand crowns, which had been a handful of potsherds. The
tombs were opened, rifled, and then filled in with earth again.
All the land proprietors with property in the neighbourhood
carried on excavations, and endless treasure was exhumed.
Within two months of the time when he started excavating,
Lucien Bonaparte had got more than two thousand Etruscan
objects out of tombs occupying a few acres of ground. That the
Etruscans should have left fortunes to the Bonapartes seems an
irony: but so it was. Vulci had mines indeed: but mostly of
painted vases, those «brides of quietness» which had been only
too much ravished[4]. The tombs have little to show now.

We ate our food, the mare cropping the grass. And I
wondered, seeing youths on bicycles, four or five, come
swooping down the trail across the stream, out of emptiness,
dismount and climb the high curve of the bridge, then disappear
into the castle. From the mountains a man came riding on an
ass: a pleasant young man in corduroy velveteens. He was riding
without a saddle. He had a word with Luigi, in the low, secretive
tones of the country, and went on towards the bridge. Then
across, two men on mules came trotting down to the bridge: and
a peasant drove in two bullocks, whose horns pricked the sky
from the tall poise of the bridge.

The place seemed very populous for so lonely a spot. And
still, all the air was heavy with isolation, suspicion, guardedness.
It was like being in the Middle Ages. I asked Luigi to go to the
house for some wine. He said he didn't know if he could get it:
but he went off, with the semi-barbaric reluctance and fear of
approaching a strange place.

[4] See fn. 7 ch. 2.

After a while he came back, to say the *dispensa* was shut, and he couldn't get any. «Then,» said I, «let us go to the tombs! Do you know where they are?» He pointed vaguely into the distance of the moorland, and said they were there, but that we should want candles. The tombs were dark, and no one was there. «Then let us get candles from the peasants,» I said. He answered again, the *dispensa* was shut, and we couldn't get candles. He seemed uneasy and depressed, as the people always are when there is a little difficulty. They are so afraid and mistrustful of one another.

We walked back to the black ruin, through a dark gateway that had been portcullised, into a half-ruined black courtyard, curiously gloomy. And here seven or eight men were squatting or standing about, their shiny bicycles leaning against the ruined walls. They were queer-looking men, youngish fellows, smallish, unshaven, dirty; not peasants, but workmen of some sort, who looked as if they had been swept together among the rubbish. Luigi was evidently nervous of them: not that they were villains, merely he didn't know them. And he had one friend among them: a queer young fellow of about twenty, in a close-fitting blue jersey, a black, black beard on his rather delicate but *gamin* face, and an odd sort of smile. This young fellow came roving round us, with a queer, uneasy, half-smiling curiosity. The men all seemed like that, uneasy and as it were outcast, but with an unknown quality too. They were, in reality, the queer, poorest sort of natives of this part of the Maremma.

The courtyard of the castle was black and sinister, yet very interesting in its ruined condition. There were a few forlorn rat-like signs of peasant farming. And an outside staircase, once rather grand, went up to what was now apparently the inhabited quarter, two or three rooms facing the bridge[5].

The feeling of suspicion and almost of opposition, negative rather than active, was still so strong we went out again and on to the bridge. Luigi, in a dilemma, talked mutteringly to his black-bearded young friend with the bright eyes: all the men

---

[5] The upper rooms and the courtyard of the castle are now host to the Archaeological Museum of Vulci.

seemed to have queer, quick bright black eyes, with a glint on them such as a mouse's eyes have.

At last I asked him, flatly: «Who are all those men?» He muttered that they were the workmen and navvies. I was puzzled to know *what* workmen and navvies, in this loneliness? Then he explained they were working on the irrigation works, and had come in to the *dispensa* for their wages and to buy things - it was Saturday afternoon - but that the overseer, who kept the *dispensa*, and who sold wine and necessaries to the workmen, hadn't come yet to open the place, so we couldn't get anything.

At least, Luigi didn't explain all this. But when he said these were the workmen from the irrigation diggings, I understood it all.

By this time, we and our desire for candles had become a feature in the landscape. I said to Luigi, why didn't he ask the *peasants*. He said they hadn't any. Fortunately at that moment an unwashed woman appeared at an upper window in the black wall. I asked her if she couldn't sell us a candle. She retired to think about it - then came back to say, surlily, it would be sixty centimes. I threw her a lira, and she dropped a candle. So!

Then the black-bearded young fellow glintingly said we should want more than one candle. So I asked the woman for another, and threw her fifty centimes - as she was contemplating giving me the change for the lira. She dropped another candle.

Brewster and I moved towards the *carretto*, with Luigi. But I could see he was still unhappy. «Do you know where the tombs are?» I asked him. Again he waved vaguely: «Over there» But he was unhappy. «Would it be better to take one of those men for a guide?» I said to him. And I got the inevitable answer: «It is as you think.» «If *you* don't know the tombs well,» I said to him, «then find a man to come with us.» He still hesitated, with that dumb uncertainty of these people. «Find a man anyhow,» I said, and off he went, feebly.

He came back in relief with the peasant, a short but strong *maremmano* of about forty, unshaven but not unclean. His name was Marco, and he had put on his best jacket to accompany us. He was quiet and determined-seeming - a brownish blond, not one of the queer black natives with the round soft contours. His boy of about thirteen came with him, and they two climbed on the back of the *carretto*.

Marco gave directions, and we bowled down the trail, then away over a slight track, on to the heathy strong moorland. After us came a little black-eyed fellow on a bicycle. We passed on the left a small encampment of temporary huts made of planks, with women coming out to look. By the trail were huge sacks of charcoal, and the black charcoal-burners, just down from the mountains, for the week-end, stood aside to look at us. The asses and mules stood dropping.

This was the winter camp of the charcoal-burners. In a week or so, Marco told me, they would abandon this camp and go up into the mountains, out of reach of the fevers which begin in May. Certainly they looked a vigorous bunch, if a little wild. I asked Marco if there was much fever - meaning malaria. He said: «Not much.» I asked him if he had had any attacks. He said: «No, never.» It is true he looked broad and healthy, with a queer, subdued, explosive sort of energy. Yet there was a certain motionless, rather worn look in his face, a certain endurance and sallowness, which seemed like malaria to me. I asked Luigi, our driver, if he had had any fever. At first he too said no. Then he admitted he had had a touch now and then. Which was evident, for his face was small and yellowish, evidently the thing had eaten into him. Yet he too, like Marco, had a strong, *manly* energy, more than the ordinary Italians. It is evidently the thing, in these parts, to deny that the malaria has ever touched you.

To the left, out of the heath, rose great flattish mounds, great tumuli, bigger than those of Cerveteri. I asked Marco were those the tombs? He said those were the tumuli, Coccumella and Coccumelletta - but that we would go first to the river tombs.

We were descending a rocky slope towards the brink of the ravine, which was full of trees, as ever. Far away, apparently, behind us to the right, stood the lonely black tower of the castle, across the moorland whence we had come. Across the ravine was a long, low hill, grass and moorland: and farther down the stream were the irrigation works. The country was all empty and abandoned-seeming, yet with that peculiar, almost ominous, poignancy of places where life has once been intense. «Where do

they say the city of Vulci was?» I asked Marco. He pointed
across stream, to the long, low elevation along the opposite side
of the ravine. I guessed it had been there - since the tombs were
on this side. But it looked very low and undefended, for an
Etruscan site: so open to the world! I supposed it had depended
upon its walls, seawards, and the ravine inland. I asked Marco if
anything was there; some sign of where the walls had gone
round. He said: «Nothing!» It has evidently not been a very large
city, like Caere and Tarquinia. But it was one of the cities of the
League, and very rich indeed, judging from the thousands of
painted vases which have been found in the tombs here.

The rocky descent was too uneven. We got out of the cart,
and went on foot. Luigi left the mare, and Marco led us on,
down to a barbed-wire fence. Marco expertly held the wire
apart, and we scrambled through on to the bushy, rocky side of
the ravine. The trees rose from the riverside, some leaves bright
green. And we descended a rough path, past the entrance-
passage to a tomb most carefully locked with an iron gate, and
defended with barbed wire, like a hermit's cave with the rank
vegetation growing up to choke it again.

Winding among rank vegetation and fallen rocks of the face
of the ravine, we came to the openings of the tombs, which were
cut into the face of the rock, and must have been a fine row
once, like a row of rock-houses with a pleasant road outside,
along the ravine. But now they are gloomy holes down which
one must clamber through the excavated earth. Once inside,
with the three candles - for the black-faced youth on the bicycle
had brought a stump too - we were in gloomy wolves' dens of
places, with large chambers opening off one another as at
Cerveteri, damp beds of rock for the coffins, and huge grisly
stone coffins, seven feet long, lying in disorder, among fallen
rocks and rubble, in some of them the bones and man-dust still
lying dismally. There was nothing to see but these black, damp
chambers, sometimes cleared, sometimes with coarse great
sarcophagi and broken rubbish and excavation-rubble left
behind in the damp, grisly darkness.

Sometimes we had to wriggle into the tombs on our bellies,
over the mounds of rubble, going down into holes like rats,

while the bats flew blindly in our faces. Once inside, we clambered in the faint darkness over huge pieces of rock and broken stone, from dark chamber to chamber, four or five or even more chambers to a tomb, all cut out of the rock and made to look like houses, with the sloping roof-tilts and the central roof-beam. From these roofs hung clusters of pale brown furry bats, in bunches, like bunches of huge furry hops. One could hardly believe they were alive, till I saw the squat little fellow of the bicycle holding his candle up to one of the bunches, singeing the bats' hair, burning the torpid creatures, so the skinny wings began to flutter, and half-stupefied, half-dead bats fell from the clusters of the roof, then groped on the wing and began to fly low, staggering towards the outlet. The dark little fellow took pleasure in burning them. But I stopped him at it, and he was afraid, and left them alone.

He was a queer fellow - quite short, with the fat, soft, round curves, and black hair and sallow face and black bats' eyes of a certain type of this district. He was perhaps twenty years old, and like a queer burrowing dumb animal. He would creep into holes in the queerest way, with his queer, soft, round hind-quarters jutting behind: just like some uncanny animal. And I noticed the backs of his ears were all scaly and raw with sores; whether from dirt or some queer disease, who can say. He seemed healthy and alive enough, otherwise. And he seemed quite unconscious of his sore ears, with an animal unconsciousness.

Marco, who was a much higher type, knew his way about, and led us groping and wriggling and clambering from tomb to tomb, among the darkness and brokenness and bats and damp, then out among the fennel and bushes of the ravine top, then in again into some hole. He showed us a tomb whence only last year they had taken a big stone statue - he showed me where it had stood, there, in the innermost chamber, with its back to the wall. And he told me of all the vases, mostly broken pieces, that he too had lifted from the dirt, on the stone beds.

But now there is nothing, and I was tired of climbing into these gruesome holes, one after another, full of damp and great fallen rocks. Nothing living or beautiful is left behind - nothing. I was glad when we came to the end of the excavated tombs, and saw beyond only the ravine bank grown over with bushes and fennel and great weeds. Probably many a vase and many a stone coffin still lie hidden there - but let them lie. We went back along the path the way we had come, to climb back to the upper level. As we came to the gangway leading to the locked tomb Marco told me that in here were paintings and some things left behind. Probably it was the famous François tomb with the paintings that are copied in the Vatican museum. It was opened by the excavator François[6] in 1857, and is one of the very, very few painted tombs found at Vulci.

We tried in vain to get in. Short of smashing the lock, it was impossible. Of course, in these expeditions, one should arm oneself with official permits. But it means having officials hanging around.

So we climbed up to the open world, and Luigi made us get into the *carretto*. The mare pulled us jolting across towards the great tumuli, which we wanted to see. They are huge grassy-bushy mounds, like round, low hills. The band of stone-work round the base, if it be there, is buried.

Marco led us inside the dense passage of brambles and bushes which leads to the opening into the tumulus. Already this passage is almost blocked up, overgrown. One has to crawl under the scratching brambles, like a rabbit.

And at last one is in the plain doorway of the tumulus itself. Here, even in 1839, two weird stone sphinxes guarded the entrance. Now there is nothing. And inside the passage or at the angles were lions and griffins on guard. What now shall we find as we follow the candelight in the narrow, winding passage? It is like being in a mine, narrow passages winding on and on, from nowhere to nowhere. We had not any great length of candle left:

---

[6] Alessandro François (1796-1857), Florentine archaeologist, the most famous of Dennis' days. Since 1819, from his residence in Portoferraio on Elba, he carried out excavations in Tarquinia, Vulci, Cosa, Roselle, Populonia, Chiusi, Cortona and Volterra, often accompanied by Nöel de Vergers, the author of *L'Etrurie et les Etrusques*(Paris, 1862-64). François' excavation reports are published on the *Bull. Corr. Archeologica* 1849-56. A famous painted tomb at Vulci, and a big Attic crater (VI C. B.C.) found at Chiusi (now at the Archaeological Museum of Florence), are still named after him. François died of malaria, which he had contracted on the field at Vulci.

four stumps. Marco left one stump burning at the junction of the passages as a signpost, and on and on we went, from nowhere to nowhere, stooping a little, our hats brushing the clusters of bats that hung from the ceiling as we went on, one after the other, pinned all the time in the narrow stone corridors that never led anywhere or did anything. Sometimes there was a niche in the wall - that was all.

There must, surely, be a central burial chamber, to which the passages finally led. But we didn't find it. And Marco said there was no such thing - the tumulus was all passages and nothing but passages. But Dennis says that when the tumulus was opened in 1829 there were two small chambers in the heart of the mound, and rising from these, two shafts of masonry which passed up to the apex of the mound, and probably these supported great monuments, probably the phallic cippi. On the floor of the chamber were fragments of bronze and frail gold[7]. But now there is nothing; the centre of the tumulus is no doubt collapsed.

It was like being burrowing inside some ancient pyramid. This was quite unlike any other Etruscan tomb we had seen: and if this tumulus was a tomb, then it must have been a very important person whose coffin formed the nut inside all this shell - a person important as a Pharaoh, surely. The Etruscans were queer people, and this tumulus, with no peripheral tombs, only endless winding passages, must be either a reminiscence of pre-historic days or of Egyptian pyramids.

When we had had enough of running along passages in nowhere we got out, scrambled through the bramble tangle, and were thankful to see clear heaven again. We all piled into the *carretto*, and the mare nobly hauled us up to the trail. The little dark fellow sailed ahead silently, on his bicycle, to open the gate for us. We looked round once more at the vast mound of the Coccumella, which strange dead hands piled in soft earth over two tiny death-chambers, so long ago: and even now it is weirdly conspicuous across the flat Maremma. A strange, strange nut indeed, with a kernel of perpetual mystery! And once it rose

---

[7] Dennis 1883 ed. I, 452 ff.

suave as a great breast, tipped with the budded monuments of
the cippi! It is too problematic. We turn our back on it all as the
carretto jolts over the tomb-rifled earth. There is something
gloomy, if rather wonderful, about Vulci.

The charcoal-burners were preparing to wash their faces for
Sunday, in the little camp. The women stood smiling as we
drove by on the moor. «Oh, how fat thou hast got!» Luigi
shouted to one plump and smiling woman. «*You* haven't
though!» she shouted back at him. «*Tu pure no!*»

At the bridge we said good-bye to Marco and his boy, then
we pulled over the arch once more. But on the other side Luigi
wanted to drink. So he and I scrambled down to the spring, the
old, thin-trickling spring, and drank cool water. The river
rushed below: the bridge arched its black, soaring rainbow
above, and we heard the shouts of mule-drivers driving the
mules over the arch.

Once this old bridge carried an aqueduct, and it is curious to
see the great stalactitic mass[8] that hangs like a beard down the
side facing the mountains. But the aqueduct is gone, the muddy
stalactitic mass itself is crumbling. Everything passes!

So we climbed up and into the *carretto*, and away went the
mare at a spanking pace. We passed the young man in
velveteens, on the donkey - a peasant from the hills, Luigi said he
was. And we met horsemen riding towards us, towards the hills,
away from Montalto. It was Saturday afternoon, with a bright
sea-wind blowing strong over the Maremma, and men travelling
away from work, on horseback, on mules, or on asses. And
some drove laden donkeys out to the hills.

«It would be a good life,» I said to Luigi, «to live here, and
have a house on the hills, and a horse to ride, and space: except
for the malaria!»

Then, having previously confessed to me that the malaria
was still pretty bad, though children often escaped it, but grown
people rarely; the fever inevitably came to shake them sometimes; that Montalto was more stricken than the open country;

---

[8] It is the so-called 'Devil's Handkerchief', an «extraordinary curtain of stalactites
which overhangs the bridge on the Northern side, depending in huge jagged masses from
the parapet» (Dennis 1883 ed. I,440). The bridge is in fact also known as 'of the Devil'.

and that in the time of rains the roads were always impassable -
one was cut off - now Luigi changed his tune: said there was
almost no fever any more; the roads were always passable; in
Montalto people came at bathing season to bathe in the sea,
having little cane huts on the coast: the roads were always
passable, easily! and that you never got fever at all if you were
properly fed, and had a bit of meat now and then, and a decent
glass of wine. He wanted me so much to come and have some
abandoned house in the foothills; and he would look after my
horses, and we would go hunting together - even out of season,
for there was no one to catch you.

Brewster dozed lightly while we drove joltingly on. It was a
dream too. I would like it well enough - if I were convinced
about that malaria. And I would certainly have Luigi to look
after the horses. He hasn't a grand appearance, but he is solitary
and courageous and surely honest, solitary, and far more manly
than the townsmen or the grubbing peasants.

So, we have seen all we could see of Vulci. If we want to see
what the Etruscans buried there we must go to the Vatican, or to
the Florence museum, or to the British Museum in London, and
see vases and statues, bronzes, sarcophagi and jewels. In the
British Museum lie the contents, for the most part, of the famous
Tomb of Isis, where lay buried a lady whom Dennis[9] thought
was surely Egyptian, judging from her statue, that is stiff and
straight, and from the statuette of «Isis», the six ostrich eggs and
other imported things that went to the grave with her: for in
death she must be what she was in life, as exactly as possible.
This was the Etruscan creed. How the Egyptian lady came to
Vulci, and how she came to be buried there along with a lady of
ancient Etruria, down in that bit of the Vulci necropolis now
called Polledrara, who knows? But all that is left of her is now in
the British Museum. Vulci has nothing. Anyhow she was surely
not Egyptian at all. Anything of the archaic East Mediterranean
seemed to Dennis Egyptian.

So it is. The site of Vulci was lost from Roman times till
1828. Once found, however the tombs were rapidly gutted by

[9] Dennis 1883 ed. I,457 ff.

the owners, everything precious was taken away, then the tombs were either closed again or abandoned. All the thousands of vases that the Etruscans gathered so lovingly and laid by their dead, where are they? Many are still in existence. But they are everywhere except at Vulci.

PLAN OF VOLTERRA, ANCIENT AND MODERN.

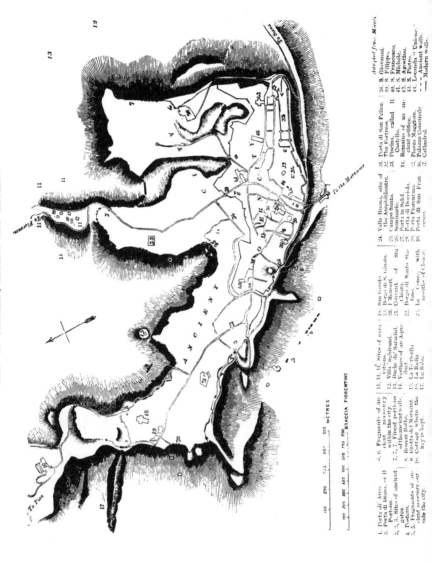

METRES
100 200 300 400 500 600 750 800

BRACCIA FIORENTINE

1. Porta dell' Arco.
2. Porta di Diana, or Il Portone.
3, 3. Sites of ancient gates.
4. Modern.
5, 5. Fragments of ancient masonry outside the city.
6, 6. Fragments of ancient masonry within the city.
7, 7. Finest portions of the ancient wall.
8. Roman Baths.
9. Grotta de' Marmini.
10. Cottage where the key is kept.
11, 11, 11. Sites of excavations.
12. Villa Inghirami.
13. Buca de' Saracini.
14. Vestiges of an Aqueduct.
15. La Torricella.
16. La Badia.
17. Le Balze.
18. San Giusto.
19. Borgo di S. Giusto.
20. Monteri.
21. Convent of Sta. Chiara.
22. Borgo di Santo Stefano.
23. La Fontana, with mouths of Cloacæ.
24. Valle Buona, site of the Amphitheatre.
25. Campo Santo.
26. Porta Marmini.
27. Porta di Solci.
28. Porta di Docciola.
29. Porta Fiorentina.
30. Porta di San Francesco.
31. Porta di San Felice.
32. The Fortress.
33. Piscina, called Il Castello.
34. Remains of an ancient edifice.
35. Piazza Maggiore.
36. Palazzo Comunale.
37. Cathedral.
38. S. Giovanni.
39. S. Filippo.
40. S. Francesco.
41. S. Michele.
42. S. Agostino.
43. S. Pietro.
44. Locanda "Unione."
— Ancient walls.
- - Modern walls.

Adapted from Menti.

6 - VOLTERRA

Volterra is the most northerly of the great Etruscan cities of the west. It lies back some thirty miles from the sea, on a towering great bluff of rock that gets all the winds and sees all the world, looking out down the valley of the Cecina to the sea, south over vale and high land to the tips of Elba, north to the imminent mountains of Carrara, inward over the wide hills of the Pre-Apennines, to the heart of Tuscany.

You leave the Rome-Pisa train at Cecina, and slowly wind up the valley of the stream of that name, a green, romantic, forgotten sort of valley, in spite of all the come-and-go of ancient Etruscans and Romans, medieval Volterrans and Pisans, and modern traffic. But the traffic is not heavy. Volterra is a sort of inland island, still curiously isolated, and grim.

The small, forlorn little train comes to a stop at the Saline di Volterra, the famous old salt works now belonging to the State, where brine is pumped out of deep wells. What passengers remain in the train are transferred to one old little coach across the platform, and at length this coach starts to creep like a beetle up the slope, up a cog-and-ratchet line[1], among the vineyards and olives you pass almost at walking-pace, and there is not a flower to be seen, only the beans make a whiff of perfume now and then, on the chill air, as you rise and rise, above the valley below, coming level with the high hills to south, and the bluff of rock with its two or three towers, ahead.

After a certain amount of backing and changing, the fragment of a train eases up at a bit of a cold wayside station,

59

---

[1] A rack railway of 8 1/2 kms. used to climb the steep ascent from Saline or Mojenuove to Volterra, from September 1912 to November 1958, when the track was finally dismantled.

and is finished. The world lies below. You get out, transfer yourself to a small ancient motor-omnibus and are rattled up to the final level of the city, into a cold and gloomy little square, where the hotel is[2].

The hotel is simple and somewhat rough, but quite friendly, pleasant in its haphazard way. And what is more, it has central heating, and the heat is on, this cold, almost icy, April afternoon. Volterra lies only 1800 feet above the sea, but it is right in the wind, and cold as any Alp.

The day was Sunday, and there was a sense of excitement and fussing, and a bustling in and out of temporarily important persons, and altogether a smell of politics in the air. The waiter brought us tea, of a sort, and I asked him what was doing. He replied that a great banquet was to be given this evening to the new *podestà* who had come from Florence to govern the city, under the new regime[3]. And evidently he felt that this was such a hugely important 'party' occasion we poor outsiders were of no account.

It was a cold, grey afternoon, with winds round the hard dark corners of the hard, narrow medieval town, and crowds of black- dressed, rather squat little men and pseudo-elegant young women pushing and loitering in the streets, and altogether that sense of furtive grinning and jeering and threatening which 60 always accompanies a public occasion - a political one especially - in Italy, in the more out-of-the way centres. It is as if the people, alabaster-workers and a few peasants, were not sure which side they wanted to be on, and therefore were all the more ready to exterminate anyone who was on the other side. This

---

[2] It's the *Albergo Nazionale* at the bottom of Piazza dei Ponti at Volterra.

[3] On April 10, 1927, a reception was held in Volterra in honour of the new *Podestà*, Colonel Carraro, who had just come into office, taking over from the former *Sindaco* Count Guidi (see *Il Corazziere* Sun 10/4/1927). Unlike the 'sindaci', the 'podestà' were institutional novelties, specially appointed by the Fascist Regime to take over local Goverments. By a curious coincidence, which perhaps didn't escape L.'s attention, on the very same day the national press gave full coverage of Mussolini's speech announcing the project of rescuing the two ancient Roman ships sunk in the lake of Nemi. The salvage, completed in 1931 thanks to a complex hydraulic machinery, was fully in in line with Mussolini's attempt to stress some purported affinity between Fascism and Imperial Rome.

fundamental uneasiness, indecision, is most curious in the Italian soul. It is as if the people could never be wholeheartedly anything: because they can't trust anything. And this inability to trust is at the root of the political extravagance and frenzy. They don't trust themselves, so how can they trust their 'leaders' or their 'party'?

Volterra, standing sombre and chilly alone on her rock, has always, from Etruscan days on, been grimly jealous of her own independence. Especially she has struggled against the Florentine yoke. So what her actual feelings are, about this new-old sort of village tyrant, the *podestà*, whom she is banqueting this evening, it would be hard, probably, even for the Volterrans themselves to say. Anyhow the cheeky girls salute one with the 'Roman' salute, out of sheer effrontery: a salute which has nothing to do with me, so I don't return it. Politics of all sorts are anathema. But in an Etruscan city which held out so long against Rome I consider the Roman salute unbecoming, and the Roman *imperium* unmentionable.

It is amusing to see on the walls, too, chalked fiercely up: *Morte a Lenin!* though that poor gentleman has been long enough dead, surely even for a Volterran to have heard of it. And more amusing still is the legend permanently painted: *Mussolini ha sempre ragione!* Some are born infallible, some achieve infallibility, and some have it thrust upon them.

But it is not for me to put even my little finger in any political pie. I am sure every post-war country has hard enough work to get itself governed, without outsiders interfering or commenting. Let those rule who can rule.

We wander on, a little dismally, looking at the stony stoniness of the medieval town. Perhaps on a warm sunny day it might be pleasant, when shadow was attractive and a breeze welcome. But on a cold, grey, windy afternoon of April, Sunday, always especially dismal, with all the people in the streets, bored and uneasy, and the stone buildings peculiarly sombre and hard and resistant, it is no fun. I don't care about the bleak but truly medieval piazza: I don't care if the Palazzo Pubblico has all sorts of amusing coats of arms on it: I don't care about the cold cathedral, though it is rather nice really, with a glow of dusky

candles and a smell of Sunday incense: I am disappointed in the
wooden sculpture of the taking down of Jesus, and the bas-
reliefs don't interest me. In short, I am hard to please.

The modern town is not very large. We went down a long,
61 stony street, and out of the *Porta all'Arco*, the famous old
Etruscan gate. It is a deep old gateway, almost a tunnel, with the
outer arch facing the desolate country on the skew, built at an
angle to the old road, to catch the approaching enemy on his
right side, where the shield did not cover him. Up handsome and
round goes the arch, at a good height, and three dark heads,
now worn featureless, reach out curiously and inquiringly, one
from the keystone of the arch bases, to gaze from the city and
into the steep hollow of the world beyond.

Strange, dark old Etruscan heads of the city gate, even now
they are featureless they still have a peculiar, out-reaching life of
their own. Ducati[4] says they represented the heads of slain
enemies hung at the city gate. But they don't hang. They stretch
with curious eagerness forward. Nonsense about dead heads.
They were city deities of some sort.

And the archaeologist says that only the door-posts of the
outer arch, and the inner walls, are Etruscan work. The Romans
restored the arch, and set the heads back in their old positions.
(Unlike the Romans to set anything back in its old position!)
While the wall above the arch is merely medieval.

But we'll call it Etruscan still. The roots of the gate, and the
dark heads, these they cannot take away from the Etruscans.
And the heads are still on the watch.

The land falls away steeply, across the road in front of the
arch. The road itself turns east, under the walls of the modern
city, above the world: and the sides of the road, as usual outside
the gates, are dump-heaps of plaster and rubble, dump-heaps of
the white powder from the alabaster works, the waste edge of
the town.

The path turns away from under the city wall, and dips
down along the brow of the hill. To the right we can see the
tower of the church of Santa Chiara, standing on a little

---

[4] Ducati 1925 II,91.

platform of the irregularly-dropping hill. And we are going there. So we dip downwards above a Dantesque, desolate world, down to Santa Chiara, and beyond. Here the path follows the top of what remains of the old Etruscan wall. On the right are little olive-gardens and bits of wheat. Away beyond is the dismal sort of crest of modern Volterra. We walk along, past the few flowers and the thick ivy, and the bushes of broom and marjoram, on what was once the Etruscan wall, far out from the present city wall. On the left the land drops steeply, in uneven and unhappy descents.

The great hilltop or headland on which Etruscan 'Volterra', *Velathri, Vlathri* once stood spreads out jaggedly, with deep-cleft valleys in between, more or less in view, spreading two or three miles away. It is something like a hand, the bluff steep of the palm sweeping in a great curve on the west and south, to seawards, the peninsulas or fingers running jaggedly inland. And the great wall of the Etruscan city swept round the south and eastern bluff, on the crest of steeps and cliffs, turned north and crossed the first finger, or peninsula, then started up hill and down dale over the fingers and into the declivities, a wild and fierce sort of way, hemming in the great crest. The modern town occupies merely the highest bit of the Etruscan city site.

The walls themselves are not much to look at, when you climb down. They are only fragments, now, huge fragments of embankment, rather than wall, built of uncemented square masonry, in the grim, sad sort of stone. One only feels, for some reason, depressed. And it is pleasant to look at the lover and his lass going along the top of the ramparts, which are now olive-orchards, away from the town. At least they are alive and cheerful and quick.

On from Santa Chiara the road takes us through the grim and depressing little suburb-hamlet of San Giusto, a black street that emerges upon the waste open place where the church of San Giusto rises like a huge and astonishing barn. It is so tall, the interior should be impressive. But no! It is merely nothing. The architects have achieved nothing, with all that tallness. The children play around with loud yells and ferocity. It is Sunday evening, near sundown, and cold.

Beyond this monument of Christian dreariness we come to the Etruscan walls again, and what was evidently once an Etruscan gate: a dip in the wall-bank, with the groove of an old road running to it.

Here we sit on the ancient heaps of masonry and look into weird yawning gulfs, like vast quarries. The swallows, turning their blue backs, skim away from the ancient lips and over the really dizzy depths, in the yellow light of evening, catching the upwards gusts of wind, and flickering aside like lost fragments of life, truly frightening above those ghastly hollows. The lower depths are dark grey, ashy in colour, and in part wet, and the whole thing looks new, as if it were some enormous quarry all slipping down.

This place is called *Le Balze* - the cliffs. Apparently the waters which fall on the heights of Volterra collect in part underneath the deep hill and wear away at some places the lower strata, so that the earth falls in immense collapses. Across the gulf, away from the town, stands a big, old, picturesque, isolated building, the *Badia* or Monastery of the Camaldolesi, sad-looking, destined at last to be devoured by *Le Balze*, its old walls already splitting and yielding.

From time to time, going up to the town homewards, we come to the edge of the walls and look out into the vast glow of gold, which is sunset, marvellous, the steep ravines sinking in darkness, the farther valley silently, greenly gold, with hills breathing luminously up, passing out into the pure, sheer gold gleams of the far-off sea, in which a shadow, perhaps an island, moves like a mote of life. And like great guardians the Carrara mountains jut forward, naked in the pure light like flesh, with their crests portentous: so that they seem to be advancing on us: while all the vast concavity of the west roars with gold liquescency, as if the last hour had come, and the gods were smelting us all back into yellow transmuted oneness.

But nothing is being transmuted. We turn our faces, a little frightened, from the vast blaze of gold, and in the dark, hard streets the town band is just chirping up, brassily out of tune as usual, and the populace, with some maidens in white, are streaming in crowds towards the piazza. And, like the band, the populace also is out of tune, buzzing with the inevitable suppressed jeering. But they are going to form a procession.

When we come to the square in front of the hotel, and look out from the edge into the hollow world of the west, the light is sunk red, redness gleams up from the far-off sea below, pure and fierce, and the hollow places in between are dark. Over all the world is a low red glint. But only the town, with its narrow streets and electric light, is impervious.

The banquet, apparently, was not till nine o'clock, and all was hubbub. Brewster and I dined alone soon after seven, like two orphans whom the waiters managed to remember in between whiles. They were so thrilled getting all the glasses and goblets and decanters, hundreds of them, it seemed, out of the big chiffonnier-cupboard that occupied the back of the dining-room, and whirling them away, stacks of glittering glass, to the banquet-room: while out-of-work young men would poke their heads in through the doorway, black hats on, overcoats hung over one shoulder, and gaze with bright inquiry through the room, as though they expected to see Lazarus risen, and not seeing him, would depart again to the nowhere whence they came. A banquet is a banquet, even if it is given to the devil himself; and the *podestà* may be an angel of light.

Outside was cold and dark. In the distance the town band tooted spasmodically, as if it were short-winded this chilly Sunday evening. And we, not bidden to the feast, went to bed. To be awakened occasionally by sudden and roaring noises - perhaps applause - and the loud and unmistakable howling of a child, well after midnight.

Morning was cold and grey again, with a chilly and forbidding country yawning and gaping and lapsing away beneath us. The sea was invisible. We walked the narrow cold streets, whose high, cold, dark stone walls seemed almost to press together, and we looked in at alabaster workshops, where 64 workmen, in Monday-morning gloom and half-awakedness, were turning the soft alabaster, or cutting it out, or polishing it.

Everybody knows Volterra marble - so called - nowadays, because of the translucent bowls of it which hang under the electric lights, as shades, in half the hotels of the world. It is nearly as transparent as alum, and nearly as soft. They peel it down as if it were soap, and tint it pink or amber or blue, and turn it into all those things one does not want: tinted alabaster lamp-shades, light-bowls, statues, tinted or untinted, vases, bowls with doves on the rim, or vine-leaves, and similar curios. The trade seems to be going strong. Perhaps it is the electric-light demand: perhaps there is a revival of interest in 'statuary'. Anyhow there is no love lost between a Volterran alabaster worker and the lump of pale Volterran earth he turns into marketable form. Alas for the goddess of sculptured form, she has gone from here also.

But it is the old alabaster jars we want to see, not the new. As we hurry down the stony street the rain, icy cold, begins to fall. We flee through the glass doors of the museum, which has just opened, and which seems as if the alabaster inside had to be kept at a low temperature, for the place is dead-cold as a refrigerator.

Cold, silent, empty, unhappy the museum seems. But at last an old and dazed man arrives, in uniform, and asks quite scared what we want. «Why, to see the museum!» «*Ah! Ah! Ah si - si!*» It just dawns upon him that the museum is there to be looked at. «*Ah si, si, Signori !*».

We pay our tickets, and start in. It is really a very attractive and pleasant museum, but we had struck such a bitter cold April morning, with icy rain falling in the courtyard, that I felt as near to being in the tomb as I have ever done. Yet very soon, in the rooms with all those hundreds of little sarcophagi, ash-coffins, or urns, as they are called, the strength of the old life began to warm one up.

Urn is not a good word because it suggests, to me at least, a vase, an amphora, a round and shapely jar: perhaps through association with Keats' *Ode to a Grecian Urn*[5] - which vessel no doubt wasn't an urn at all, but a wine-jar - and with the 'tea-urn' of children's parties. These Volterran urns, though correctly enough used for storing the ashes of the dead, are not round,

---

[5] See fn. 7 ch 2.

they are not jars, they are small alabaster sarcophagi. And they are a peculiarity of Volterra. Probably because the Volterrans had the alabaster to hand.

Anyhow here you have them in hundreds, and they are curiously alive and attractive. They are not considered very highly as 'art'. One of the latest Italian writers on Etruscan things, Ducati (1925 II,110), says: «If they have small interest from the artistic point of view, they are extremely valuable for the scenes they represent, either mythological or relative to the beliefs in the after-life.»

George Dennis, however, though he too does not find much 'art' in Etruscan things, says of the Volterran ash-chests. «The touches of Nature on these Etruscan urns, so simply but eloquently expressed, must appeal to the sympathies of all - they are chords to which every heart must respond; and I envy not the man who can walk through this museum unmoved, without feeling a tear rise in his eye,

And recognising ever and anon
The breeze of Nature stirring in his soul.»
(Dennis 1883 ed. II,185)

The breeze of Nature no longer shakes dewdrops from our eyes, at least so readily, but Dennis is more alive than Ducati to that which is alive. What men mean nowadays by 'art' it would be hard to say. Even Dennis said that the Etruscans never approached the pure, the sublime, the perfect beauty which Flaxman reached. Today, this makes us laugh: the Greekified illustrator of Pope's *Homer*! But the same instinct lies at the back of our idea of 'art' still. Art is still to us something which has been well cooked - like a plate of spaghetti. An ear of wheat is not yet 'art'. Wait, wait till it has been turned into pure, into perfect macaroni.

For me, I get more real pleasure out of these Volterran chests than out of - I had almost said, the Parthenon frieze. One wearies of the aesthetic quality - a quality which takes the edge off everthing, and makes it seem 'boiled down'. A great deal of pure Greek beauty has this boiled-down effect. It is too much cooked in the artistic consciousness.

In Dennis's day a broken Greek or Greekish amphora would

fetch thousands of crowns in the market, if it was the right 'period', etc. These Volterran urns fetched hardly anything. Which is a mercy, or they would be scattered to the ends of the earth.

As it is, they are fascinating, like an open book of life, and one has no sense of weariness with them, though there are so many. They warm one up, like being in the midst of life.

The downstairs rooms of ash-chests contain those urns representing 'Etruscan' subjects: those of sea-monsters, the sea-man with fish-tail, and with wings, the sea-woman the same or the man with serpent-legs, and wings, or the woman the same. It was Etruscan to give these creatures wings, not Greek.

73 If we remember that in the old world the centre of all power was at the depths of the earth, and the depths of the sea, while the sun was only a moving subsidiary body: and that the serpent represented the vivid powers of the inner earth, not only such powers as volcanic and earthquake, but the quick powers that run up the roots of plants and establish the great body of the tree, the tree of life, and run up the feet and legs of man, to establish the heart: while the fish was the symbol of the depths of the waters, whence even light is born: we shall see the ancient power these symbols had over the imagination of the Volterrans. They were a people faced with the sea, and living in a volcanic country.

Then the powers of the earth and the powers of the sea take life as they give life. They have their terrific as well as their prolific aspect.

Someone says the wings of the water-deities represent evaporation towards the sun, and the curving tails of the dolphin represent torrents. This is part of the great and controlling ancient idea of the come-and-go of the life-powers, the surging up, in a flutter of leaves and a radiation of wings, and the surging back, in torrents and waves and the eternal downpour of death.

Other common symbolic animals in Volterra are the beaked griffins, the creatures of the powers that tear asunder and, at the same time, are guardians of the treasure. They are lion and eagle combined, of the sky and of the earth with caverns. They do not allow the treasure of life, the gold, which we should perhaps translate as consciousness, to be stolen by thieves of life. They are guardians of the treasure: and then, they are the tearers asunder of those who must depart from life.

It is these creatures, creatures of the elements, which carry men away into death, over the border between the elements. So is the dolphin, sometimes; and so the hippocampus, the sea-horse; and so the centaur.

The horse is always the symbol of the strong animal life of man and sometimes he rises, a sea-horse, from the ocean: and *67* sometimes he is a land creature, and half-man. And so he occurs on the tombs, as the passion in man returning into the sea, the soul retreating into the death-world at the depths of the waters: or sometimes clothed in a lion-skin, to show his dread aspect, bearing the soul back, away, off into the other-world.

It would be very interesting to know if there were a definite connection between the scene on the ash-chest and the dead whose ashes it contained. When the fish-tailed sea-god entangles a man to bear him off, does it mean drowning at sea? And when *71* a man is caught in the writhing serpent-legs of the Medusa, or of the winged snake-power, does it mean a fall to earth; a death from the earth, in some manner; as a fall, or the dropping of a rock, or the bite of a snake? And the soul carried off by a winged centaur: is it a man dead of some passion that carried him away?

But more interesting even then the symbolic scenes are those scenes from actual life, such as boar-hunts, circus-games, processions, departures in covered wagons[6], ships sailing away, city gates being stormed, sacrifice being performed, girls with open scrolls, as if reading at school; many banquets with man and woman on the banqueting couch, and slaves playing music, and children around: then so many really tender farewell scenes, the dead saying good-bye to his wife, as he goes on the journey, or as the chariot bears him off, or the horse waits; then the soul alone, with the death-dealing spirits standing by with their hammers that gave the blow. It is as Dennis says, *the breeze of*

---

[6] It is the *carpentum, -i*, a two-wheeled covered wagon, used in towns by women also, or a small country cart.

Nature stirs one's soul. I asked the gentle old man if he knew anything about the urns. But no! no! He knew nothing at all. He had only just come. He counted for nothing. So he protested. He was one of those gentle, shy Italians too diffident even to look at the chests he was guarding. But when I told him what I thought some of the scenes meant he was fascinated like a child, full of wonder, almost breathless. And I thought again, how much more Etruscan than Roman the Italian of today is: sensitive, diffident, craving really for symbols and mysteries, able to be delighted with true delight over small things, violent in spasms, and altogether without sternness or natural will-to-power. The will-to-power is a secondary thing in an Italian, reflected on to him from the Germanic races that have almost engulfed him.

The boar-hunt is still a favourite Italian sport, the grandest
53 sport of Italy. And the Etruscans must have loved it, for they represent it again and again, on the tombs. It is difficult to know what exactly the boar symbolised to them. He occupies often the
68 centre of the scene, where the one who dies should be: and where the bull of sacrifice is. And often he is attacked, not by men, but by young winged boys, or by spirits. The dogs climb in the trees around him, the double axe is swinging to come down on him, he lifts up his tusks in a fierce wild pathos. The archaeologists say that it is Meleager and the boar of Calydon, or Hercules and the fierce brute of Erymanthus. But this is not enough. It is a symbolic scene: and it seems as if the boar were himself the victim this time, the wild, fierce fatherly life hunted down by dogs and adversaries. For it is obviously the boar who must die: he is not, like the lions and griffins, the attacker. He is the father of life running free in the forest, and he must die. They say too he represents winter: when the feasts for the dead were held. But on the very oldest archaic vases the lion and the boar are facing each other, again and again, in symbolic opposition.

70   Fascinating are the scenes of departures, journeyings in covered wagons drawn by two or more horses, accompanied by driver on foot and friend on horseback, and dogs, and met by other horsemen coming down the road. Under the arched tarpaulin tilt of the wagon reclines a man, or a woman, or a whole family and all moves forward along the highway with

wonderful slow surge. And the wagon, as far as I saw, is always drawn by horses, not by oxen.

This is surely the journey of the soul. It is said to represent even the funeral procession, the ash-chest being borne away to the cemetery, to be laid in the tomb. But the *memory* in the scene seems much deeper than that. It gives so strongly the feeling of a people who have trekked in wagons, like the Boers, or the Mormons, from one land to another.

They say these covered-wagon journeys are peculiar to Volterra, found represented in no other Etruscan places. Altogether the feeling of the Volterran scenes is peculiar. There is a great sense of *journeying*: as of a people which remembers its migrations, by sea as well as land. And there is a curious restlessness, unlike the dancing surety of southern Etruria: a touch of the Gothic.

In the upstairs rooms there are many more ash-chests, but mostly representing Greek subjects: so called. Helen and the Dioscuri, Pelops, Minotaur, Jason, Medea fleeing from Corinth, 69 Oedipus and the Sphinx, Ulysses and the Sirens, Eteocles and 71 Polynices, Centaurs and Lapithae, the Sacrifice of Iphigenia - all are there, just recognisable. There are so many Greek subjects that one archaeologist suggested that these urns must have been made by a Greek colony planted there in Volterra after the Roman conquest.

One might almost as well say that *Timon of Athens* was written by a Greek colonist planted in England after the overthrow of the Catholic Church. These 'Greek' ash-chests are about as Grecian as *Timon of Athens* is. The Greeks would have done so much 'better'. No, the 'Greek' scenes are innumerable, but it is only just recognisable what they mean. Whoever carved these chests knew very little of the fables they were handling: and fables they were, to the Etruscan artificers of that day, as they would be to the Italians of this. The story was just used as a peg upon which the native Volterran hung his fancy, as the Elizabethans used Greek stories for their poems. Perhaps also the alabaster cutters were working from old models, or the memory of them. Anyhow, the scenes show nothing of Hellas.

Most curious these 'classic' subjects: so unclassic! To me

they hint at the Gothic which lay unborn in the future, far more than at the Hellenistic past of the Volterran Etruscan. For, of course, all these alabaster urns are considered late in period, after the fourth century B.C. The Christian sarcophagi of the fifth century A.D. seem much more akin to these ash-chests of Volterra than do contemporary Roman chests: as if Christianity really rose, in Italy, out of Etruscan soil, rather early, a glad sort of Christian art, the free touch of Gothic within the classic, seems evident in the Etruscan scenes. The Greek and Roman 'boiled' sort of form gives way to a raggedness of edge and a certain wildness of light and shade which promises the later Gothic, but which is still held down by the heavy mysticism from the East.

Very early Volterran urns were probably plain stone or terracotta. But no doubt Volterra was a city long before the Etruscans penetrated into it, and probably it never changed character profoundly. To the end, the Volterrans burned their dead: there are practically no long sarcophagi of Lucumones. And here most of all one feels that the *people* of Volterra, or Velathri, were not Oriental, not the same as those who made most show at Tarquinii. This was surely another tribe, wilder, cruder, and far less influenced by the old Aegean influences. In Caere and Tarquinii the aborigines were deeply overlaid by incoming influences from the East. Here not! Here the wild and untamable Ligurian was neighbour, and perhaps kin, and the town of wind and stone kept, and still keeps, its northern quality.

So there the ash-chests are, an open book for anyone to read who will, according to his own fancy. They are not more than two feet long, or thereabouts, so the figure on the lid is queer and stunted. The classic Greek or Asiatic could not have borne that. It is a sign of barbarism in itself. Here the northern spirit was too strong for the Hellenic or Oriental or ancient Mediterranean instinct. The Lucumo and his lady had submit to being stunted, in their death-effigy. The head is nearly life-size. The body is squashed small.

But there it is, a portrait-effigy. Very often, the lid and the chest don't seem to belong together at all. It is suggested that the lid was made during the lifetime of the subject, with an attempt at real portraiture: while the chest was bought ready-made, and apart. It may be so. Perhaps in Etruscan days there were the alabaster workshops as there are today, only with rows of ash-chests portraying all the vivid scenes we still can see: and perhaps you chose the one you wished your ashes to lie in. But more probably, the workshops were there, the carved ash-chests were there, but you did not select your own chest, since you did not know what death you would die. Probably you only had your portrait carved on the lid, and left the rest to the survivors.

So maybe, and most probably, the mourning relatives hurriedly *ordered* the lid with the portrait-bust, after the death of the near one, and then chose the most appropriate ash-chests. Be it as it may, the two parts are often oddly assorted: and so they were found with the ashes inside them. But we must believe that the figure on the lid, grotesquely shortened, is an attempt at a portrait. There is none of the distinction of the southern Etruscan figures. The heads are given the «imperious» tilt of the Lucomones, but here it becomes almost grotesque. The dead nobleman may be wearing the necklace of office and holding the sacred *patera* or libation-dish in his hand; but he will not, in the southern way, be represented ritualistically as naked to below the navel; his shirt will come to his neck; and may just as well be holding the tippling wine-cup in his hand as the sacred patera; he may even have a wine-jug in his other hand, in full carousal. Altogether the peculiar «sacredness», the inveterate symbolism of the southern Etruscans, is here gone. The religious power is broken.

It is very evident in the ladies: and so many of the figures are ladies. They are decked up in all their splendour, but the mystical formality is lacking. They hold in their hands wine-cups or fans or mirrors, pomegranates or perfume-boxes, or the queer little books which perhaps were the wax tablets for writing *71* upon. They may even have the old sexual and death symbol of the pine-cone. But the *power* of the symbol has almost vanished. The Gothic actuality and idealism begins to supplant the profound *physical* religion of the southern Etruscans, the true ancient world.

In the museum there are jars and bits of bronze, and the *patera* with the hollow knob in the middle. You may put your two middle fingers in the *patera*, and hold it ready to make the last libation of life, the first libation of death, in the correct Etruscan fashion. But you will not, as so many of the men on these ash-chests do, hold the symbolic dish upside down, with the two fingers thrust into the *mundum*[7]. The torch upside down means the flame has gone below, to the underworld. But the *patera* upside down is somehow shocking. One feels the Volterrans, or men of *Velathri*, were slack in the ancient mysteries.

At last the rain stopped crashing down icily in the silent inner courtyard; at last there was a ray of sun. And we had seen all we could look at for one day. So we went out, to try to get warmed by a kinder heaven.

There are one or two tombs still open, especially two outside the *Porta a Selci*. But I believe, not having seen them, they are of small importance. Nearly all the tombs that have been opened in Volterra, their contents removed, have been filled in again, so as not to lose two yards of the precious cultivable land of the peasants. There were many tumuli: but most of them are levelled. And under some were curious round tombs built of unsquared stones, unlike anything in southern Etruria. But then, Volterra is altogether unlike southern Etruria.

One tomb has been removed bodily to the garden of the archaelogical museum in Florence: at least its contents have. There it is built up again as it was when discovered in Volterra in 1861, and all the ash-chests are said to be replaced as they stood originally. It is called the *Inghirami Tomb*, from the famous Volterran archaelogist Inghirami[8].

A few steps lead down into the one circular chamber of the

---

[7] See fn. 6 ch. 2.

[8] Cavalier Francesco Inghirami (b. 1772 - d. 1846), author of the fundamental 10 volumes of *Monumenti Etruschi* (1820-1826), which he personally edited and illustrated. George Dennis too (1883 ed. II,127) paid a visit to this «patriarch of Etruscan antiquaries» at «La Badia, a quaint old abbey at the foot of the hill of Fiesole, long his residence.»

tomb, which is supported in the centre by a square pillar, apparently supposed to be left in the rock. On the low stone bed that encircles the tomb stand the ash-chests, a double row of them, in a great ring encircling the shadow.

The tomb belongs all to one family, and there must be sixty ash-chests, of alabaster, carved with the well-known scenes. So that if this tomb is really arranged as it was originally, and the ash-chests progress from the oldest to the latest counter-clockwise, as is said, one ought to be able to see certainly a century or two of development in the Volterran urns.

But one is filled with doubt and misgiving. Why, oh why, wasn't the tomb left intact as it was found, where it was found? The garden of the Florence museum is vastly instructive, if you want object-lessons about the Etruscans. But who wants object-lessons about vanished races? What one wants is a contact. The Etruscans are not a theory or a thesis. If they are anything, they are an *experience*.

And the experience is always spoilt. Museums, museums, museums, object-lessons rigged out to illustrate the unsound theories of archaeologists, crazy attempts to co-ordinate and get into a fixed order that which has no fixed order and will not be co-ordinated! It is sickening! Why must all experience be systematized? Why must even the vanished Etruscans be reduced to a system? They never will be. You break all the eggs, and produce an omelette which is neither Etruscan nor Roman nor Italic nor Hittite, nor anything else, but just a systematized mess. Why can't incompatible things be left incompatible? If you make an omelette out of a hen's egg, a plover's, and an ostrich's, you won't have a grand amalgam or unification of hen and plover and ostrich into something we may call «oviparity». You'll have that formless object, an omelette.

So it is here. If you try to make a grand amalgam of Cerveteri and Tarquinia, Vulci, Vetulonia, Volterra, Chiusi, Veii, then you won't get the essential *Etruscan* as a result, but a cooked-up mess which has no life-meaning at all. A museum is not a first-hand contact: it is an illustrated lecture. And what one wants is the actual vital touch. I don't want to be «instructed»; nor do many other people.

They could take the more homeless objects for the museums, and still leave those that *have* a place in their own place: the Inghirami Tomb here at Volterra.

But it is useless. We walk up the hill and out of the Florence gate, into the shelter under the walls of the huge medieval castle which is now a State prison. There is a promenade below the ponderous walls, and a scrap of sun, and shelter from the biting wind. A few citizens are promenading even now. And beyond, the bare green country rises up in waves and sharp points, but it is like looking at the choppy sea from the brow of a tall ship; here in Volterra we ride above all.

And behind us, in the bleak fortress, are the prisoners[9]. There is a man, an old man now, who has written an opera inside those walls. He had a passion for the piano: and for thirty years his wife nagged him when he played. So one day he silently and suddenly killed her. So, the nagging of thirty years silenced, he got thirty years in prison, and *still* is not allowed to play the piano. It is curious.

There were also two men who escaped. Silently and secretly they carved marvellous likenesses of themselves out of the huge loaves of hard bread the prisoners get. Hair and all, they made their own effigies lifelike. Then they laid them in the bed, so that when the warder's light flashed on them he should say to himself: «There they lie sleeping, the dogs!»

And so they worked, and they got away. It cost the governor, who loved his houseful of malefactors, his job. He was kicked out. It is curious. He should have been rewarded, for having such clever children, sculptors in bread.

---

[9] Pino Orioli, the first publisher of *Lady Chatterley's Lover* (1928) is probably the source of the following anecdotes on the *Maschio*, the old Volterran penitentiary. The same stories are found in his *Adventures of a Bookseller* (1934).

LAWRENCE IN ETRURIA: *ETRUSCAN PLACES* IN CONTEXT.
by Giovanni Kezich

(translated by John Gatt)

I got home all right on Monday night - pretty well shaken up, after five hours in that bus. But I caught the last tram, by the skin of my teeth. ... I liked our Etruscan trip so much. Pity it was so short. When I feel more myself, I am going to try doing some sketches. The country between Volterra and San Gemignano is very queer and empty - very hilly in sharp little hills, and rather bare, and no villages. (14/4/1927)

These words come from a letter which D.H. Lawrence wrote to his friend and travelling companion, Earl Brewster, on 14 April 1927, a few days after his return to Scandicci. It had been a long-standing desire of Lawrence to visit the Etruscan sites along the Tyrrhenian coast:

Also, will you tell me *what* then was the secret of the Etruscans, which you saw written so plainly in the place you went to? please don't forget to tell me, as they do rather puzzle me, the Etruscans.(25/10/1921)

he wrote from Taormina in 1921 to Catherine Carswell, his friend and later his biographer, who may perhaps be identified as one of the party who made the trip to Tarquinia described by Aldous Huxley in *Those Barren Leaves* (1925). Carswell's reply couldn't have been an exaustive one, seeing that Lawrence kept reading for years about the topic - a constant interest of English visitors to Italy - and decided to go and check in person shortly after returning to Italy from his long trip around the world that had taken him to Ceylon as the Brewsters' guest, to Australia and to Mexico (1922-1925). At the start of 1927, Earl Brewster and his wife Achash also returned to their home in Ravello after a long sojourn in the East where they had gone to study Buddhism and the Pali texts. Brewster, whom Lawrence had met on Capri in 1921, was a wealthy young American, a self-styled painter, passionately interested in oriental mysticism. Lawrence, at first drawn to theosophy and mysticism, then increasingly sceptical, shared his own speculations on the subject with him.

As was his wont, Lawrence satirized Brewster in a jocular *Apostrophe to a Buddhist Monk* and, more sharply, in the brief tale *Things* (1926). In their cordial diatribes together, the Etruscans were often brought into play:

> I am reading about the Etruscans, and looking at their remains. They interest me. I suppose they are the dead opposite of Buddha: but not of Brahma or Shiva (16/5/1926) ... I've got a book on the Bagh caves - not nearly so thrilling as the Ajanta caves - but interesting. Did you know that in ancient Buddhism the *stupa* occupied the holy central position in the cave, or the temple: and when the Buddha figure was invented, the *standing* Buddha took the place of this stupa. ... In later days Lawrence often used to say of the seated Buddha: 'Oh I wish he would *stand up!*' (Brewster 1934;49) Now it looks to me as if this stupa was just the monumental phallic symbol, like the Etruscan *cippus*. And the standing Buddha has still a phallic quality. They invented the seated one later. ... (8/11/1926)

At the start of 1927, the two friends were at last able to arrange for this long-desired tour:

> Brewster, as a man sympathetic to mysticism, was an ideal companion for this journey: that sympathy was to Lawrence both a stimulus and a check, for he was free to let himself go, imaginatively, and at the same time he was just suspicious enough of Brewster, as a confirmed mystic, not to let himself go too far. A sceptic would have been unbearable: the gentle, sometimes agreeing, sometimes disagreeing, New England Brewster was precisely the right fellow voyager. (Moore 1955; 364)

From Villa Mirenda at Scandicci, where he had been staying for six months or so, Lawrence met up with his friend at Sorrento and they set out together on their brief trip, first stopping in Rome to see the Etruscan holdings in the Villa Giulia Museum, then, from Wednesday 6th to Monday 11th April, 1927, going through the Etruscan Places. Brewster retained a pleasant memory of the trip:

Volterra - Natale di Roma
21 Aprile 1924

59. *The rack-and-pinion train from Saline to Volterra (8 1/2 km.),
established in 1912 and removed in 1958.*

60. *Volterra. Festival of the Foundation of Rome in the Piazza dei
Priori.*

61. Porta all'Arco, mid 3rd to 2nd century B.C., in a photograph of the Twenties.

62. *Volterran milk-vendors with their typical country hat of grey felt, at Porta Marcoli in the Twenties.*

63. *The Volterra Balze, facing west.*

64. Alabaster workshop in the Twenties.

MUSEO GUARNACCI = VOLTERRA

Sono pregati i signori visitatori a lasciar memoria di
sè apponendo in quest'albo la loro firma coll'indicazione
dei titoli, professioni e patria.

La Direzione sarà grata agli Archeologi se vorranno
aggiungere apprezzamenti ed osservazioni tendenti ad illustrare
ed interpretare i monumenti.

Volterra, li 11 Aprile 1927

D.H. Lawrence
scrittore - inglese
E.H. Brewster - pittore Americano

65. *Lawrence at the Museo Guarnacci: autograph.*

66. *Volterra alabaster urns, Museo Guarnacci. Figure on cover no.
219, showing strong Hellenistic influence. Late 3rd to early 2nd century
B.C. Note the* patera umbilicata *held in the right hand.*

67. Urn no. 57. Chest with allegorical figure: the carved relief of the
chest shows the sun-chariot over the sea. Early 2nd century B.C.

68. Urn no. 321. The chest depicts the hunt of the Calydonian Boar.
Second half of the 2nd century B.C.

69. Urn no. 330. *The figure on the cover is holding a* rhython *in its right hand and a* patera umbilicata, *face down, under the third and fourth fingers of its left hand. The chest depicts Andromeda at the mercy of the sea-monster, and Perseus. From the middle of the 2nd century B.C.*

70. Urn no. 141. Aulus Caecina Selcia, the boy on the cover, died at the age of 12. The chest, of uncertain attribution, shows the journey into the underworld by carpentum. After 90 B.C.: Etruria now speaks Latin.

71. *Urn no. 183. The deceased on the cover is holding a pomegranate and a writing diptych. The chest depicts the rape of Proserpine, with a winged demon, and a sea-serpent. Dated to around the mid 2nd century B.C.*

72. *The Inghirami Tomb, discovered in 1861 and reconstructed shortly after in the garden of the Museo Archeologico in Florence. Used by the Ati family for a little over 100 years, from the beginning of the 2nd century B.C.*

73. *Lawrence and Frieda depicted as Boreas and Orythia, following the Graeco-Etruscan model Eos and Kephalos, by Anna Mirenda, their hostess. Fresco in the villa's entrance hall, circa 1927.*

74. *Villa Mirenda at San Polo near Scandicci, Lawrence's home from may 1926 until may 1928.*

75. *D.H. Lawrence and Aldous Huxley in Tuscany.*

76. *D.H. Lawrence, 1927.*

From Sorrento we started on our Etruscan Pilgrimage, beginning with the Museum of the Villa di Papa Giulio in Rome. With what lively interest Lawrence studied its treasures! In his writings on the Etruscan cities he has described our visits to Cerveteri, Tarquinia, Grosseto and Volterra. I have not read all of those articles: I wonder if he describes our long drive from Montalto to Vulci, through the wildest country I have seen in Italy. The road crosses the ancient one-arched Ponte dell'Abbadia. The vast half-ruined abbey beside it, far from any other dwelling, was occupied by a few families who were most hesitant in having anything to do with us, even to selling us candles for the tombs. Yet when we went in to those excavations the whole male population accompanied us and patiently waited for us outside each underground chamber until we emerged.

How happy were our days at Tarquinia! The tombs are on a high plateau back a few miles from the sea. They number about a hundred and cover the area of a small city. We were thrilled by the freshness and beauty of their mural paintings. I felt Lawrence truly maintained Etruscan art has a certain sensitive quality not found in the Greek. The symbolism, as he explained it, seemed so convincing that I could but wonder at the variety of explanations archaeologists give to it. From the jewelled splendour of those dark tombs we came forth into the brightness of an April day and a blue sky, broken by hurrying white clouds: the fields through which we walked were gay with red poppies: our guide unlocked the door leading to another tomb and we would descend again to behold the joyous scenes with which the Etruscans, of such a distant world, chose to decorate the homes of their dead. For hours we continued these alternations between past and present. Late that afternoon we took a long walk, into the valley below the plateau of Tarquinia and climbed to the top of a neighbouring hill. We made bold plans for the future, I at least a little suspecting how soon Lawrence would lose even the strength he then possessed. Perhaps those were the last long walks he took.

My memory is that Easter morning found us at Grosseto (*note: it was Palm Sunday, April 10th, 1927 at Volterra): there we passed a little shop, in the window of which was a toy white rooster escaping from an egg. I remarked that it suggested a title - «The Escaped Cock - a story of the Resurrection». (Brewster 1934; 122- 3)

Three weeks later, Lawrence announced to Brewster that he had written

> a story of the Resurrection, where Jesus gets up and feels very sick about everything, and can't stand the old crowd anymore - so cuts out - and as he heals up, he begins to find what an astonishing place the phenomenal world is, far more marvellous than any salvation or heaven - and thanks his stars he needn't have a «mission» anymore. It's called *The Escaped Cock* from that toy in Volterra. Do you remember?

In the second part of this story, which also appeared under the title *The Man Who Had Died*, the protagonist, like a true hero of antiquity, is received by a priestess of Isis in her temple sheer above the sea, where the disappointed Messiah and the frustrated Vestal waste little time in coming round to that same elemental creed that Lawrence had made his own and which he felt he had divined in the funerary figurations of the Etruscans. This takes us into Lawrence's final phase - that of *The Plumed Serpent* (1926) and *Mornings in Mexico* (1927), of *Lady Chatterley's Lover* (1928) and of *Apocalypse* (1931) - where his drift becomes more and more explicit. Following both the non-religious interpretation proffered in James Frazer's *The Golden Bough* (1911) and the theosophic approach of J.M. Pryse's *The Apocalypse Unsealed*, the Christ of *The Escaped Cock* is Osiris, the pagan symbol of the natural cycle of death and rebirth, as was also Quetzalcoatl, the 'plumed serpent' of the Aztecs, and also like the Phoenix, reborn out of its own ashes, by now a favourite emblem of the writer's.

> Rebecca West saw him as wandering like the Indian Fakir and the Russian Saint, going on journeys with a spiritual rather than a geographical goal: 'Lawrence travelled, it seemed, to get a certain Apocalyptic vision of mankind that he registered again and again and again, always rising to a pitch of ecstatic agony'. (Moore 1955; 280)

Lawrence's Etruscan «pilgrimage» fits into this same pattern:

> There was an ancestral symbolism in the descent of the

collier's son into these underground places, led by a guide with a lamp or a candle that cast a glare onto the stuccoed walls painted in reds and blacks and yellows showing dancers and hunters and bulls and lions. Lawrence loved the Etruscans, who were both a «dark» people and a sun people. They had no false literary culture and lived in the phallic consciousness, knowing «the everlasting *wonder* of things». (Moore 1955; 364)

Richard Aldington, Lawrence's friend and biographer, writes:

> Lawrence's return to Tuscany was fortunate. I think he always liked it, and was as happy at the Mirenda as anywhere, except perhaps the Ranch and Sicily. Boccaccio, who is the very essence of country Tuscany, was one of the few authors he always loved, a man filled with that warm instinctive life Lawrence wanted so much to see around him. And for a long time he had had a hankering to investigate the Etruscans for himself, and to write a book about them.
> The Etruscans were quite a godsend. Here was a lost European civilization which had never been guilty of a Homer or Plato, and had no extant literature at all. There is no history of the Etruscans, for the book about them by the Emperor Claudius has disappeared, and the dislike of the Romans for a conquered and perhaps more civilized people, added to Christian horror of 'pagans', has left us little but archaeology and conjecture. To increase their attractiveness, you will find that the Etruscans are not favourites of the learned, who accuse them of immorality and of borrowing what culture they had from other races. They were a very religious people, greatly interested in the divine significance of the flight of birds and of the entrails of sacrifices. They must have believed in some sort of life after death, since they constructed cities of elaborate tombs planned in imitation of their towns, burying their dead in full armour or festival robes in painted chambers filled with precious objects and offerings to the dead. Sometimes the dead were burned, and placed in carved marble or alabaster coffers.
> Lawrence believed that Etruscan art had a quality of its own, quite different from Greek or Roman art; and what he found there and liked so much was that intense 'physical' life he thought the world has very nearly lost. The Etruscans did not possess much 'aesthetic' feeling, the Greek love of

perfection, harmony, grace. They were wonderful craftsmen in gold, for the best modern goldsmiths cannot quite equal the delicacy of their filigree work. The best of their bronzes have great spirit and energy - for example, the chariots and shields in the Vatican, and the elongated statuettes in Florence. The Apollo of Veii at the Villa di Papa Giulio and the tomb in the British Museum show what they could achieve in terracotta. Almost more important are the wall-paintings and the carved stone caskets of the dead. On or near every Etruscan tomb was a conventionalized phallus - a symbol of the triumph of life over death. Some of the later wall-paintings have horrid devils of death in them, but most of the earlier ones are rather gay. They depict the life of the living, and there are real warmth and tenderness in the love scenes. Moreover, those carved figures of obese magistrates and often ugly men and women have extraordinary vitality. They fascinate an attentive observer, in Rome and Florence, in Volterra, Perugia, Orvieto - even in the smallest collection.

All this you know as well as I; but the point I want to stress is the depth to which Lawrence was stirred by these vestiges of a lost civilization. For my present purpose, it is irrelevant to ask whether Lawrence had or had not any 'scientific' basis for Etruscan enthusiasm. What matters is that he found in the Etruscans (or lent them, it doesn't matter) a conception of life such as he believed in himself. Perhaps it is only a poet's dream, a transference to the remote past of an ideal he despaired of finding in the present. This conception comes up again in *Apocalypse*, and indeed runs through much of his work. In *Apocalypse* the Etruscans have fallen into the background, as a rather belated specimen of the 'great Aegean civilization' which existed before 1000 B.C., of which the Etruscans are quite possibly an off-shoot. Whether imagined or not, here at least were civilizations which Lawrence felt he could love, nations of men and women living an intense 'physical' life without too much restless intellect and hatred. And in Etruria at any rate the women enjoyed great liberty and consideration, while the idea of sex and sexual desire as shameful things had never been thought of - that was an importation of the puritan Romans.

... I think Lawrence had the sweetest imagination and feeling about sex of any man I have known; just as, in its essential meaning, he was a truly 'religious' man. ... But I must add one little story to show how sensitive Lawrence was to anything which he thought at all vulgar or indelicate in these

matters. One day we were spelling out Etruscan inscriptions -
you know, they go from right to left. I transcribed *A.R.S.E.*
Lawrence scratched his head and said, 'I wonder what that
means, Richard?' I said, 'Well, I don't know what it means in
Etruscan, but I know what it means in English.' How cross he
was with me! Afterwards he said to someone else, 'You know,
I used to think Richard was sound, but now I'm afraid he is
just like other Englishmen!«

... The Etruscan book had been in his mind for a long
time, and he died without finishing it. I thought the manuscript (it has not yet been published) extremely interesting, less
perhaps for what it told me about the Etruscans (though that
is stimulating enough) than for what it told me about
Lawrence. To put it roughly in a sentence, Lawrence believed
that the Etruscans of about 700-300 B.C. had lived largely in
the way he wished to live and thought that we should all live.
The Etruscans were a great convenience, for, since nobody
knows much about them, nobody could contradict what he
said.(Aldington 1932)

Nevertheless, Lawrence read thoroughly both in preparation
for the trip and for the writing of his book. He sent for many
works on the Etruscans from the London Library as long as a
year earlier and delved into George Dennis's fine volumes of *The
Cities and Cemeteries of Etruria* (1848, and republished in 1883 -
though Lawrence may have had the 1907 pocket edition) and the
very detailed and up-to-date ones of Pericle Ducati's *Etruria
Antica* (1925). The illustrations in Fritz Weege's *Etruskische
Malerei* (1921), which his mother-in-law obtained for him in
Germany, and some plates expressely ordered from the Alinari
Archives -

We've been lent Weege's book on the tombs - all the
illustrations - very interesting indeed. I got photographs too
from Alinari - and on the one from the *Tomba dei Tori*, the
two little improper bits, *un poco pornografico*, as brave as
life. Amusing! (3/5/1927)

That helped him to refresh his memory in describing the
painted tombs, and his descriptions are in fact photographically
precise, all the figures arrayed in their correct position, with

never a slip.

For over a year Lawrence continued to nurse the hope of a second trip -

> I want to go etruscanizing at the end of this week - weather being decent

- a fortnight with Frieda and with Huxley, who had been in Tarquinia in the early Twenties. He wanted to follow the complete route taken by Dennis:

> Meanwhile I think I shall go to Arezzo and Cortona, Chiusi, Orvieto, Perugia with Frieda, towards the end of next week. I'd like to go to those places before we leave. With Cerveteri and Tarquinia, Vulci and Volterra, that makes nine of the great cities - the twelve. But it leaves a whole bookful of little places - Veii, Civita Castellana, Norchia, Vetulonia, Cosa, Populonia, Bieda - we might do those, and make a second volume - after.

He had planned to write a book of a dozen essays and 80,000 words in length (cf. Fussel 1980; 162). But, mostly because of his deteriorating health, neither the tour nor the book were completed.

In the meantime, Lawrence began in June 1927 to draft his travelogue for the magazines *Travel* and *The World Today* -

You see they *have* to go in a *picture* magazine (21/10/1927)

Travel carried three articles:*City of the Dead at Cerveteri* (Nov.1927), *Ancient Metropolis of the Etruscans* (Dec. 1927), and *The Windswept Strongholds of Volterra*, while *The World Today* published a series of four articles collectively entitled *Sketches of Etruscan Places* (I: *Cerveteri*; II:*Tarquinia*; III:*The Painted Tombs of Tarquinia*; IV:*Volterra* - Feb.- May 1928). Martin Secker produced the book from this material, with some cuts and some insertions of passages not previously published, in 1932, two years after the writer's death. He also included a score of the Alinari plates, which have been retained in later editions though they are not all relevant to Lawrence's account.

The result is a rich text, both composite and complex, but journalistic in style, in which meticulous descriptions alternate with inspirational passages of varying effectiveness, sometimes even cryptic, and with sudden and inexplicable lapses in tone:

> But I think I shall have to go back to Italy in December to finish those Etruscan essays - they nag at me for them - publishers always want a «book». ... But the *Sunday Dispatch* gives me £ 25 for a 2,000 article, written in an hour and a half. ... (24/11/1928)

Etruscan Places has not so far proven a great success, particularly in Italy. The critics have virtually ignored it, except for the passages I have quoted here, which are mere droplets in the great sea of Lawrence criticism. Etruscologists have mostly snubbed the work, there has been up to now been only one Italian translation, that entitled *Luoghi Etruschi*, by Lorenzo Gigli, which appeared, without illustrations, in Volume X of the *Opere Complete* of D.H. Lawrence under the general editorship of Piero Nardi (1961).

It doesn't, in fact, take much to sense that *Etruscan Places* appeals more to the sensibility of English speakers than to Italians. The Etrurian quest, inspired and motivated by a complex of attitudes and conceptions, has been for at least two centuries - and much longer, if we take as its originator Thomas Dempster, author of the seven Latin volumes of *De Etruria Regali*, published in Pisa in 1616 and 1619 and rediscovered in Rome a century later by Sir Thomas Coke - one of the fixed points of the culture of the English in Italy, a kind of baton handed on from one generation to the next of the English literary community resident in Italy, and particularly in Florence. It involves the all-embracing perception of a deep-seated substratum, untouched by a succession of imposed dominions - most signally, that of the Romans - or by the Catholic establishment: the tenacious root of the continuity of the original Italy, pre-Roman and pre-Christian, which, by convention and, as it were, as a matter of course, is to be sought on Etruscan soil.

It was such attitudes that encouraged educated Englishmen, on the eve of the *Risorgimento*, to suggest a reinterpretation of Italian cultural identity in Etruscan terms. This phase saw one of its decisive moments in the auction of a whole consignment of Etruscan antiquities, «exported» from Italy by the brothers Campanari of Tuscania, which was held in Pall Mall in 1838 and elicited a petition, signed by a great number of literary people, urging the British Museum to acquire the entire collection. Other decisive points came with the Etruscan travels of Mrs. Hamilton Gray, who wrote *Tour of the Sepulchres of Etruria* (1839) and, of course, those of George Dennis (1848), followed by *Etruscan Bologna: A Study* (1876) by Sir Richard Burton, who also discovered the Zagreb Mummy, and Frederick Seymour's *Up Hill and Down Dale in Ancient Etruria* (1910), to name only the more important contributions. By the late nineteenth century, even a critic as alert and influential as John Ruskin was seriously maintaining that

> Every line of the Florentine chisel of the fifteenth century is based on national principles of art which existed in the seventh century before Christ; and Angelico, in his convent of St. Dominic at the root of the hill of Fiesole, is as true an Etruscan as the builder who laid the rude stones of the wall along its crest. (1881; 1907 ed.90-1n.)

whilst an inveterate eclectic like Charles Leland combed the mountains of Tuscany for improbable Etruscan survivals in the local lore (*Etruscan Roman Remains in Popular Tradition*, 1893).

In *Etruscan Places*, the English cult of Etruria reaches its literary acme: in the tomb paintings of Tarquinia and the urns of Volterra as described by Lawrence, we seem to reach the fulfilment of the dream which had inspired Macaulay's *Lays of Ancient Rome* (1848) or James Frazer's researches, the quest to discern, through the forms of the classic imagination, a vital content qualitatively different from that of Rome's triumphant imperial hegemony. Lawrence's anthropology is in this sense completely *qualitative*: rather than looking for regularities and stylistic norms, his interest lies always in catching the «quick»: that unique something, inimitable and incomparable, that exists in every form of human life, whether individual or collective:

> Lawrence ranged pretty far both in space and time in the search of other modes of living which could be used either as

symbols for expressing his faith or as sticks to beat the moderns. He found bits of what he wanted in German and Italian peasants, in Mexicans and Indians. You remember how he liked the fishermen at Lavandou, going out in boats, playing boules, and eating *bouillabaisse* with their wives? (Aldington 1932)

When Brewster moralistically quoted at him a phrase of Hume's -

«It is universally acknowledged that there is a great uniformity among the actions of men, in all nations and ages, and that human nature remains still the same, in its principles and operations.»

- Lawrence had replied

As for Mr. Hume: Ambition, avarice, self-love ... the *words* are all the same: the actuality is *so* different in each individual as to make the statement feeble. (1921)

confronting his *bald head / cranium / duck-egg* friend with an unconventional polytheism of his own, certainly more Hindu than Buddhist, all blood and matter. Lawrence's conceptions, however, always appear rooted in an absolutely irrational perception of culture which is in no wise accessible to enquiry since it is based, in the final analysis, upon an esoteric theory of the nature of civilization, a theory of aristocratic or hieratic dye or, worse, upon racist tenets:

Lawrence talked much of racial differences, of those existing in the present, and of those between the present and the past. He attached much importance to actual difference of blood, which he considered affected consciousness - that is, that consciousness and the blood are more closely related than is generally recognized to-day. The elephant especially interested him as the remnant of another age. (Brewster 1934; 48)

In fact, even a well-balanced and well-disposed biographer like H.T. Moore (1955) cannot help remarking that:

This mixture of Mme. Blawatsky, Frobenius, James Pryse, and others of similar persuasions, with a belief in such things as a lost Atlantis and its irretrievable cultural priesthood ... is the most difficult and sometimes the most exasperating component of Lawrence's mysticism; it is not persistently intrusive, though at times it becomes annoying. (Moore 1955; 445)

However, it is this same biographer who reminds us soon after that

The remaining part of the prophetic in Lawrence is the most authentic and the best integrated of them all. It comprehends the values of our world, not in any abstruse mystical way nor yet in the easy rationalism of newspaper articles, but rather in the larger integration with imaginative values - the dramatization, the full embodiment, the fictional orchestration, of a long familiar, deeply felt theme. With Lawrence, this was his opposition to the mechanical forces threatening the natural: "blood-knowledge" would bring about that balance which life needs, which philosophers in their various ways strive after. And it is this Lawrence, celebrating the whole man–not the man fragmented by industrialism or money quests or mechanized love–who is the true prophetic Lawrence, bringing all his forces into play. (Moore, 1955 445-6)

Certainly, there have been some, such as Sri Aurobindo who have chosen to see in Lawrence's quest that of «a Yogi who had missed his way and come into a European body to work out his difficulties» (cf. Moore 1955; 288). But for all his endeavour in these fine pages to render to us the civilization of the Etruscans in its vivid wholeness, in all its poetic depth, Lawrence was well aware that

«We make a mistake forsaking England and moving out into the periphery of life. After all, Taormina, Ceylon, Africa, America - as far as *we* go, they are only the negation of what we ourselves stand for and are: and we're rather like Jonahs running away from the place we belong». (Moore 1955; 289)

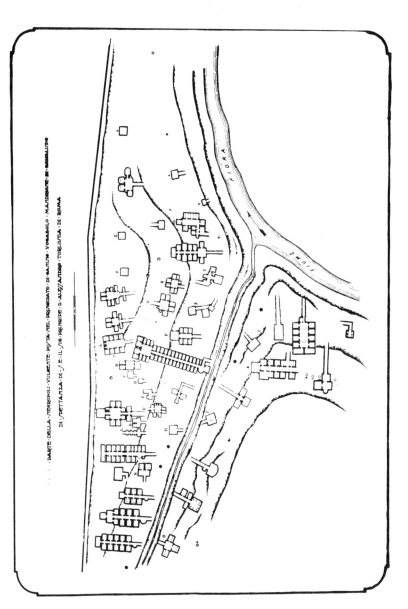

PIANTE DELLA NECROPOLI VULCENTE POSTA NEL FRUMENTO DI SATURNO E VOLABOLO MAIDEBATE DI GABELLUPO

DI DETTAGLIA DI IL PRINCIPE DI ALE ANDRO TORLONIA DI ROMA

VULCI AND ITS NECROPOLIS.

Bibliography

1. Etruscan civilization.

Dennis, G. *The Cities and Cemeteries of Etruria* 2 vols. 1st publ. London, 1848 (then 1876; 1883; 1907)

Ducati, P. *Etruria Antica* Torino, 1925

Pallottino, M. *Etruscologia* Milano, 1985 (7th ed.)

Weege, F. *Etruskische Malerei* Niemeyer, 1921

Wellard, J. *The Search for the Etruscans* London, 1973

2. D.H. Lawrence

Aldington, R. *Introduction to »Apocalypse«* London, 1932
—, *Portrait of a genius, but ... The life of D.H. Lawrence 1885-1930* London, 1950

Brewster, E. & A. *D.H. Lawrence. Reminiscences and Correspondence* London, 1932

Fussel, P. *Abroad. British literary travelling between the wars.* New York, 1980

Huxley, A. *Those Barren Leaves* London, 1925
—, *Point counter Point* London,
—, *Lawrence in Etruria* 'Spectator' 4/11/1932

Lawrence, D.H. *The Plumed Serpent* London, 1926
—, *The Escaped Cock* Black Sun Press, 1929 also as *The Man Who Had Died* Martin Secker London, 1931
—, *The Letters* edited by A. Huxley London, 1932

Lawrence, Frieda *Not I, but the wind ...* New York, 1934
Moore, H.T. *The Intelligent Heart. The story of D.H. Lawrence.* London, 1955

Orioli, P. *Adventures of a Bookseller* 'Lungarno Series' 12 - Firenze, 1934

Sources of the illustrations:

Archivi Brogi and other period sources:
8 9 12 20 21 27 28 29 33 34 42

Fabio Fiaschi - Volterra
67 68 69 70 71 72

Renato Galli - Volterra
59 60 64 65

Mauro Galeotti - Viterbo
50 51 59

Istituto Archaeologico Germanico - Roma
6 7 10 16 18 19 22 24 25 26 30 31 32 36 37 38 39 40 41 43 44 45 54 61
63 66

Soprintendenza Antichità Etruria Meridionale - Roma
1 2 3 4 5 11 49

Enio Staccini - Tuscania
55 56 57

Archivi Valerioti - Tarquinia
13 14 15 17 46 47 48 52

Various contemporary sources - all rights reserved to *nuova immagine editrice*
23 35 58 62 73 74 75 76

D. H. Lawrence
Sea and Sardinia
(pp. 208, 36 photographs, £ 20.000)

1921: from Etna to Vesuvius, in a boat across the Tyrrhenian Sea
and into the heart of Sardinia: the peregrinations of Lawrence
and his "Queen Bee", far from the tourist itinerary of those days,
through an Italy lacerated and exhausted by the effects of war.
«The most charming work he ever wrote and by far the best
introduction to his *œuvre... Sea and Sardinia...* a small miracle
of a book... a wonderful self-portrait
shows Lawrence at his most attractive.»
Anthony Burgess *Flame into being.*

Alan Dundes – Alessandro Falassi
La Terra in Piazza
An Interpretation of the Palio of Siena
(pp. 268, 112 photographs, £ 30.000)

The combination of an insider with an outsider has produced a
book which is as enjoyable as it is illuminating
(and suggests a possible future direction for anthropology)
(Peter Burke, *TLS*).

[...] For the substance and the meaning of the race,
described in a remarkable study, [...] it is nothing less than an
expression of the soul of the city, endlessly rich in symbol,
metaphor, and life [...] written with felicity and excitement.
(L.A. Times)